EXAMINING THE BIG PICTURE

*Evaluating Existentialism, Truth
And
The Meaning of Life*

Richard Wolf

Copyright © 2003 by Richard Wolf

ISBN 0-7414-1570-4

Published by:

PUBLISHING.COM

519 West Lancaster Avenue
Haverford, PA 19041-1413
Info@buybooksontheweb.com
www.buybooksontheweb.com
Toll-free (877) BUY BOOK
Local Phone (610) 520-2500
Fax (610) 519-0261

Printed in the United States of America

Printed on Recycled Paper

Published May 2003

Dedication

To my students. Every semester they inspire and challenge me to be an authentic individual.

To my wife, who faithfully took the dog out – night after night – so I could write this book. And for twenty-one great years together.

To my kids, Ashley and Ricky. Thank you for being the greatest kids this universe has ever known.

dat panis coelicus
figuris terminum

CONTENTS

Chapter One

   - *Either the world is a mere hotch-potch of random cohesions and dispersions, or else it is a unity of order and providence. If the former, why wish to survive in such a purposeless and chaotic confusion; why care about anything, save the manner of the ultimate return to dust; why trouble my head at all; since, do what I will, dispersion must overtake me sooner or later? But if the contrary be true, then I do reverence, I stand firmly, and I put my trust in the directing Power.*
                                         - Marcus Aurelius, Meditations

   The most important statements in life always come in the form of a question. The more simple the question, the more profound the insight. Take for example three elementary reflections: "Who am I?" "Why am I here?" "Where am I going?" It can be argued that the whole of philosophy is nothing more than individuals trying to answer this trinity of questions. In this sense, I believe one can reasonably argue that there is only one *genuine* school of philosophical thought - the branch of philosophy known as existentialism with its emphasis on individual meaning.
   Existentialism is a philosophical movement that believes in concrete experience over intellectual abstractions and individuality over mass culture with an emphasis on authentic living.[1] To this end, existentialism is a method of examination that demonstrates life is a quest for values and purpose.

---

[1] William F. Lawhead, *The Philosophical Journey* (Mountain View, Mayfield, 2000), 183.

1

Existential thought emphasizes individual responsibility, choice, and transparency, and imparts a sense of urgency into the reader that is often absent in other philosophical schools. Thus, far from being a movement that is out of date or unique only to the coffeehouses of Europe, existentialism continues to serve as the most potent magnifying glass of philosophical inquiry.

Whether one studies philosophy in terms of epistemology, ethics, language, or metaphysics, one is always examining these fields in relation to his individual existence and meaning. As H. J. Blackham once observed, "The peculiarity of existentialism...is that it deals with the separation of man from himself and from the world, which raises the questions of philosophy...The main business of this philosophy therefore is not to answer the questions which are raised but to drive home the questions themselves until they engage the whole man and are made personal, urgent, and anguished...Thus, existentialism goes back to the beginning of philosophy and appeals to all men to awaken from their dogmatic slumbers and discover what it means to become a human being."[2] Existentialism, therefore, with its relentless array of personal questions, stands far above other systems of thought with the inherent ability to cause individuals to examine their life for purpose and content.

The influential Russian novelist, Leo Tolstoy, demonstrated this point when he described how he found it impossible to escape from the question of the meaning and purpose of life. Tolstoy stated, "What is life for? To die? To kill myself at once? No, I am afraid. To wait for death till it comes? I fear that even more. Then I must live. But for what? In order to

---

[2] Colin Chapman, *The Case for Christianity* (Grand Rapids, Eerdmans, 1981), 210.

die?"[3] Similarly, the writer of the ancient book of Ecclesiastes, perhaps the most significant existential work ever penned, wondered aloud in chapter seven, "How can anyone discover what life means? It is too deep for us, too hard to understand?" Yet, indeed, it is the oasis of existential thought, with its continual emphasis on pursuing mankind's meaning and purpose, that truly guides one on this journey for truthfulness and authenticity. Consequently, whether one is studying Plato, Aristotle, Heidegger, Sartre, Kierkegaard or any other philosopher, one is inevitably partaking from the existential banquet of questions and answers.

The three previously basic, yet penetrating questions that I spoke of earlier ("Who am I?" "Why am I here?" "Where am I going?") – I affectionately term these as "The Big Picture" – generally receive little examination in today's classrooms or coffee shops. There is any number of reasons for this, but perhaps the most far-reaching explanation is our present willingness to abandon *Truth*. In defining the concept of truth, I simply mean belief in a binding, universal, and objective order – as opposed to the idea of relativism where all propositions are equal and each person is the sole determiner of reality. Nowhere is this *lack* of philosophical inquiry more evident than in the classroom – whether in the elementary schools or the hallowed halls of the university. The retreat from truth is one of the great dramatic, untold stories of history. For professional academics to have grown indifferent to truth is an extraordinary reversal of traditional obligations – like physicians renouncing the obligation to sustain life.[4]

---

[3] Colin Chapman, *The Case for Christianity* (Grand Rapids, Eerdmans, 1981), 15.
[4] Felipe Fernandez-Armesto, *Truth, A History and a Guide for the Perplexed* (New York, Thomas Dunne, 1997), 165.

3

What makes this retirement from truthfulness so devastating is that it – truth – is inexorably united with *meaning and purpose.* According to the absolute apologist Chuck Colson, this retreat from truth has resulted in individual and societal decay and confusion. In his address at the University of Chicago in 1993, Colson remarked, "When a society abandons its transcendent values, each individual's moral vision becomes purely personal and finally equal. Society becomes merely the sum total of individual preferences, and since no preference is morally preferable, anything that can be dared will be permitted."[5] Consequently, if man loses his ability to define and distinguish truth, he concurrently becomes unable to detect and define meaning. As Felipe Fernandez-Armesto, current member of the Modern History Faculty of Oxford University points out, "Unless *there is* (absolute or universal) truth, what status is left for a statement like 'X is wrong' where X is, say, adultery, infanticide, euthanasia, drug-dealing, Nazism, pedophilia, sadism or any other wickedness due, in today's climate, for relativization into the ranks of the acceptable. It becomes, like everything else in western society today, a matter of opinion; and we are left with no moral basis for encoding some opinions rather than others, except the tyranny of the majority."[6] Fernandez-Armesto fittingly concludes, the death of truth is upon us as a civilization "if the very distinction between truth and falsehood is abandoned as a meaningless curio (ancient artifact) of a pedantic past."[7]

Yet, there was a time when the ancient masters of philosophy – Plato and Aristotle – tutored their

---

[5] Chuck Colson, *Chuck Colson Speaks* (Uhrichsville, Promise Press, 2000), 10.
[6] Felipe Fernandez-Armesto, *Truth, A History and a Guide for the Perplexed* (New York, Thomas Dunne, 1997), 165-6.
[7] Felipe Fernandez-Armesto, *Truth, A History and a Guide for the Perplexed* (New York, Thomas Dunne, 1997), 194.

students day after day on matters of meaning, purpose, existence, life, death, justice, virtue, and most of all, truth. They could, in fact, teach on these subjects because there was a fundamental belief in the existence of objective *Truth* as a real entity – in other words, *Truth* did actually exist and was transcendent or above mere personal opinion. These giants of philosophical thought believed that realities like virtue, truth, justice, as well as others, did indeed have concrete meaning. In laying a foundation for this type of philosophical contemplation, Aristotle commented that, "To say of what is that it is, and of what is not that it is not, is truth." When Aristotle said this, he certainly meant that there is a reality which exists independently of how we, or any number of us, or any individual creatures, perceive or conceive it.[8] Several hundred years later, the champion of medieval philosophy, Thomas Aquinas, echoed Aristotle's sentiments when he proclaimed, "Truth is found in the mind when it apprehends a thing as it is." Devoted lovers of wisdom through the ages have concurred with these ancient masters and, along with William Hazlitt, boldly declared that "the contemplation of truth and beauty *is* the proper object for which we were created."

The glory of the writings of many of the ancient philosophers is that these men dared to exclaim that one could *know* what justice, virtue or truth is. There were, argued many venerable orators, certain absolutes and, contrary to modern thought, these absolute standards did not burden an individual but, rather, they reassured a person that he could find meaning because there *was* meaning to be found. In fact, as many astute thinkers throughout the ages have pointed out, philosophical absolutes actually provide a base from which all other theories and speculations

---

[8] Felipe Fernandez-Armesto, *Truth, A History and a Guide for the Perplexed* (New York, Thomas Dunne, 1997), 216-217.

can spring – a necessary foundation. As C. S. Lewis brilliantly noted, "How had I got this idea of 'just' and 'unjust'? A man does not call a line crooked unless he has some idea of a straight line."

Underscoring the need to reacquaint modern man with the existence of absolute or objective *Truth*, author Fernandez-Armesto writes, "We need a history of truth. We need to be able to tell whether truth is changeful or eternal, embedded in time or outside it, universal or varying from place to place. We need to know how we have got to where we are in the history of truth – how our society has come to lose faith in the reality of it and lose interest in the search for it."[9] Herein lies the crux of philosophy – the age-old philosophical dilemma of whether or not there is such a thing as *Truth* and, if there is, does *Truth* change and open itself up to countless interpretations? Again, Fernandez-Armesto affirms, "We need a history of truth to illuminate the unique predicament of our times and – if possible – help us escape from it. We also need it because truth is fundamental to everything else. Everyone's attempt to be good – every attempt to construct happy relationships and thriving societies – starts with two questions: How do I tell right from wrong? And how do I tell truth from falsehood?"[10]

Without a doubt, the question of *Truth* is the most critical and practical aspect of philosophical inquiry worthy of man's pondering. As the English philosopher C. E. M. Joad once stated, "The object of philosophy, as I conceive it, is not to help people, but to discover truth."[11] The magnitude of such a discovery cannot be overstated – namely, the answer to whether

---

[9] Felipe Fernandez-Armesto, *Truth, A History and a Guide for the Perplexed* (New York, Thomas Dunne, 1997), 2.
[10] Felipe Fernandez-Armesto, *Truth, A History and a Guide for the Perplexed* (New York, Thomas Dunne, 1997), 3.
[11] Colin Chapman, *The Case for Christianity* (Grand Rapids, Eerdmans, 1981), 20.

or not there is *Truth* in the universe will influence not only every one of our ideas and theories, but more importantly, our everyday actions. Take for example our basic understanding and analysis of the physical universe in which we live. Scientists are fond of making bold proclamations of truth or facts based upon what they have observed or tested. However, genuine reflection about the universe and her laws, in an existential manner, leads one initially to study the field of physical science from the perspective of *truth* and *meaning*, as opposed to charts, numbers, and tables.

Thus, an existential seeker is more likely to comprehend, as renowned intellectual Phillip Johnson has pointed out in his work, *The Right Questions*, that the study of science must begin with proper sequence. In other words, science must initiate its quest of properly understanding the universe by first acknowledging that it is not, in itself, the sum total. As apologist C. S. Lewis suggested, "Supposing science ever became complete so that it knew every single thing in the whole universe. Is it not plain that the questions, "Why is there a universe?" "Why does it go on as it does?" "Has it any meaning?" would remain just as they were?"[12] Next, science must philosophically admit that only two possible views about the universe exist. According to Johnson, either the universe or her scientific laws operate in a blind, undirected and random manner, *or* they function because of intelligent and purposeful design. It is only *after* one has resolved which of these possibilities is true that one is now able sufficiently to interpret any data observed. However, as C. S. Lewis once noted, one must take great care in making grand pronouncements based only on what one can observe. He writes, "The position of the question, then, is like

---

[12] C. S. Lewis, *Mere Christianity* (New York, Touchstone, 1952), 32-33.

this. We want to know whether the universe simply happens to be what it is for no reason *or* whether there is a power behind it that makes it what it is. Since that power, if it exists, would be not one of the *observed* facts but a reality which makes them, no mere observation of the facts can find it."[13] This is just one example that illustrates how the discipline of existential thought is the purest form of philosophical study because it does not allow one to be content with what one merely observes or senses. In fact, existentialism drives the theorist beyond chalkboard speculation and forces one to investigate all issues in relation to truth and meaning.

By placing enormous emphasis upon personal reflection within the context of purpose, existentialism shines as the premier school of thought that harmonizes an individuals beliefs and actions by stressing such concepts as choice, uniqueness, and identity. Consequently, existential thought stands alone as the most potent and valid form of self-examination that can aid a person in evaluating one's thoughts, actions, and motives with regards to his relationship with the universe. In fact, a careful study of the history of philosophy will lead one to the conclusion that existential thought, far from being "invented" by Soren Kierkegaard or Jean-Paul Sartre, has been part of humanity ever since man first pondered his existence. Whether one looks back to the ancient book of Ecclesiastes or upon the paintings on the inside of primitive caves, one is overwhelmed by the evidence of man seeking answers to his questions about his own purpose and mortality.

The distinguished Austrian psychiatrist Victor Frankl, who survived four inhumane World War II concentration camps, wrote that it is precisely this

---

[13] C. S. Lewis, *Mere Christianity* (New York, Touchstone, 1952), 33.

"search for meaning" that separates man from all other forms of life. He pointedly stated in his extraordinary work, *Man's Search for Meaning*, "The striving to find meaning in one's life is the primary motivational force in man. That is why I speak of a *will to meaning* in contrast to the pleasure principle (or, as we could also term it, the *will to pleasure*) on which Freudian psychoanalysis is centered."[14] In creating a new division of existential thought called, *logotherapy* (logos from the Greek defined as 'meaning'), Frankl taught that individuals should place great emphasis on their future actions and perceptions. He writes, "It is one of the basic tenets of logotherapy that man's main concern is not to gain pleasure or to avoid pain but rather to see a meaning in his life. That is why man is even ready to suffer, on the condition, to be sure, that his suffering has a meaning."[15]

Yet, Frankl cautions against aimlessly evaluating one's existential predicament. He admonishes his readers, "One should not search for an abstract meaning of life. Everyone has his own specific vocation or mission in life to carry out a concrete assignment that demands fulfillment. Therein he cannot be replaced, nor can his life be repeated. Thus, everyone's task is as unique as is his specific opportunity to implement it...Ultimately, man should not ask what the meaning of his life is, but rather he must recognize that it is *he* who is asked. In a word, each man is questioned by life; and he can only answer to life by *answering for* his own life; to life he can only respond by being responsible." Frankl concludes, "This emphasis on responsibleness is reflected in the categorical imperative of logotherapy, which is: Live as

---

[14] Victor Frankl, *Man's Search for Meaning* (New York, Washington Square Press, 1959), 121.
[15] Victor Frankl, *Man's Search for Meaning* (New York, Washington Square Press, 1959), 136.

if you were living already for the second time and as if you had acted the first time as wrongly as you are about to act now...Such a precept confronts him with life's *finiteness* as well as the *finality* of what he makes out of both his life and himself."[16]

This intense desire to find significance actually propels man to live his life in a unique and reflective manner – which is to say in an existential manner. Such an individual is capable of persisting in life's pilgrimage, despite the many trials and disappointments that are sure to come. Again, Frankl asserts, "There is nothing in the world, I venture to say, that would so effectively help one to survive even the worst conditions as the knowledge that there is a meaning in one's life."[17] This journey to find meaning and truth in one's life presupposes that *truth and meaning* exist and is available for discovery. Contrary to Sartre, Nietzsche, and other secular existentialists, who declare that man must endure individual existence with the knowledge that there is no ultimate purpose, Frankl replies that life not only has meaning, but, in fact, "super-meaning." Frankl writes, "This ultimate meaning necessarily exceeds and surpasses the finite intellectual capacities of man; in logotherapy, we speak in this context of a super-meaning. What is demanded of man is not, as some existential philosophers teach, to endure the meaninglessness of life, but rather to bear his incapacity to grasp its (life's) unconditional meaningfulness in rational terms. *Logos* (meaning) is deeper than logic."[18]

Yet, history is full of those who remain unsure or unconvinced of universal design, purpose, and truth.

---

[16] Victor Frankl, *Man's Search for Meaning* (New York, Washington Square Press, 1959), 131-132.

[17] Victor Frankl, *Man's Search for Meaning* (New York, Washington Square Press, 1959), 126.

[18] Victor Frankl, *Man's Search for Meaning* (New York, Washington Square Press, 1959), 141.

Nowhere is this more evident than in the post-modern age in which we live. As Christopher Dawson has said, "The Western mind has turned away from the contemplation of the absolute and eternal to the knowledge of the particular and the contingent. It has made man the measure of all things and has sought to emancipate human life from its dependence on the supernatural."[19] Therefore, generation after generation has seemingly continued to wonder whether life is a mere game possessing no cosmic intention or collection of constant rules or truths. As author, Thomas Howard succinctly asked in the preface of his work, *Chance or the Dance?*, "Is it chance or dance that moves the world? Is the world blind and dumb or bloom and festal? A vain jest, or holy feast?" Howard continues by commenting that it took the "Age of Enlightenment" to broadly convince mankind that universal truth was obsolete and unnecessary. As Howard puts it, "The myth sovereign in the *old age* (the age of belief in universal and unchangeable Truth) was that everything means everything. The myth sovereign in the *new age* (the age of belief that all truth is relative and subject to change) is that nothing means anything.[20] Because of this wholesale rejection of universal or absolute truth, the relationship between rationality and meaning has been lost. Philosopher Francis Schaeffer put it this way, "The *downstairs* has no relationship to meaning: the *upstairs* no relationship to reason. Rationalistic man, having given up the methodology of antithesis (if a thing is true, the opposite is not true), has been forced to a nonunified concept of knowledge, and consequently to a resultant

---

[19] Colin Chapman, *The Case for Christianity* (Grand Rapids, Eerdmans, 1981), 175.
[20] Thomas Howard, *Chance or the Dance?* (San Francisco, Ignatius Press, 2001), 12.

monstrous total antithesis between rationality and meaning.[21]

In chapter five of *Chance or the Dance?*, Howard laments the natural consequence that follows from embracing the post-modern myth of a purposeless and random existence. He astutely concludes, "This is a world from which significance seems to have disappeared...Things don't *mean* anything; they simply are, and the effort to keep significance alive is nostalgia or atavism. And, ironically, this disappearance of significance is the main burden of nearly all twentieth-century painting and poetry and drama...Hence we are lost. Alienated. Disfranchised. Forlorn...From these shards we must try to reconstruct something – a new pattern, a pattern with Man for a maker, since the old Maker has perished like the Titans, a pattern that will exhibit our awareness of forlornness and meaninglessness..."[22]

Sadly, but not surprisingly, the results of ignoring Victor Frankl's wisdom – that individuals have purpose and occupy a universe that also has meaning and design – have been devastating. The acceptance of the myth that man and his world are without direction or purpose has had an equally poisoning effect upon common sense and common knowledge. Not only has man been separated from order and function, but his assuredness about *any* truths has also been stripped away. When it comes to the area of knowledge, many have simply asked, "How can we know anything for certain?" As the famed mathematician Bertrand Russell voiced, "Is there any knowledge in the world which is so certain that no reasonable man could doubt

---

[21] Francis Schaeffer, *The Complete Works of Francis Schaeffer, Volume One* (Wheaton, Crossway Books, 1982), 58.
[22] Thomas Howard, *Chance or the Dance?* (San Francisco, Ignatius Press, 2001), 74-75.

it?"[23] This love affair with skepticism – the notion that we cannot be certain of anything – along with the mindless embracing of its tenants, led American philosopher Francis Schaeffer to arrive at an interesting conclusion about the current condition of cynical humanity. According to Schaeffer, "The modern man has both feet firmly planted in midair."[24]

---

[23] Coin Chapman, *The Case for Christianity* (Grand Rapids, Eerdmans, 1981), 20.
[24] Chuck Colson, *Chuck Colson Speaks* (Uhrichsville, Promise Press, 2000), 115.

Chapter Two

*- One of the things this book does for our culture
is to show...our radical distinctiveness from all previous
cultures.   The most radically new feature of our
civilization is not technology...but the lack of a
summum bonum, an end. We are the first civilization
that does not know why we exist.*

*- Peter Kreeft on his work,
"C.S. Lewis for the Third Millennium"*

Despite modern man's denial of certainty, the
search for universal or objective truth has a long history
that lies at the very heart of philosophy and existential
study. The pre-Socratic philosophers, also perplexed
by variation within the universe, generally asked if all
things – including *Truth* itself – were subject to change
(or flux). If not, was all change merely an illusion?
Philosophy students are well acquainted with the way
some of the ancient thinkers examined this issue of
truth and change. Despite many individual differences,
these philosophers were driven by a belief that a single
substance existed as the source of all things. The
rational thought that followed was that in order to
comprehend truth and the world around us one must
first understand the single substance that held the
universe together. When one comprehended that
substance, one could conceivably unlock the secrets of
the universe and answer whether or not if things in this
world were subject to change.

Thus, great debate began over what that *one*
substance was and whether or not that *one* substance
changed form in any way. Great thinkers all offered
their opinions: Thales, and his proposal that water was

the key to the universe; Anaximander, his "boundless cosmic soup" and theory of opposites; Anaximenes, who focussed on the importance of air; and the mathematical-minded Pythagoras who stressed numbers and the harmony of numerical ratios. Philosophy at this point in ancient history, and indeed still somewhat today, was deadlocked in this debate over substance, truth, and change from two very distinct perspectives. On the one side stood Hesiod and his famous *Theogony*, stating that one must look to the Divine for ultimate answers. In the 8th century BC, he wrote, "The universe is a moral order with an impersonal force controlling changes." Clearly, Hesiod, and thinkers like him, represented the side of philosophy that was concerned with questions of *WHO* created the one crucial substance of the universe and *WHY* was this substance and universe created at all? The other school of philosophy, represented by the Milesian philosophers, was more concerned with science, matter and the physical aspects of the universe. They asked *WHAT* is this universe made up of and *HOW* did the world come into being? Philosophy was in a match between the *WHY's* and the *WHAT's*.

Yet, both sides sought to solve the dilemma by striving to find the answer to one simple question – "Do things change?" Heraclitus opined that all nature is constantly changing – or in a state of continual change. This sentiment was epitomized in his famous statement, "One can never step into the same river twice." The rational behind this thought is that the moment one puts his *other* foot into the river, the river has *changed* due to the moving water. Representing the Eleatic philosophers, Parmenides countered with "What is, is, and what is not, is not." Simply stated, Parmenides was voicing the opinion that all *change* is actually an illusion because reality is one substance that will not and can not change. Consequently, although the Nile River water *moved* after one placed his foot into it, it is still, nonetheless, the Nile River that one is stepping into with his other foot – it did not suddenly *change* into the Mississippi River. Thus, as Parmenides' student Zeno would show through his famous "Paradoxes," division of reality is not possible and mere movement is not sufficient proof of change.

Now one might wonder why this elementary question of *change* was so important to these brilliant minds. Perhaps it was because if these thinkers believed that reality – all things – were subject to change, then why not *Truth* as well. In addition, if truth itself was subject to change, then how could anyone know anything with certainty? Would man be able to say that two plus two is *always* four; that murdering another human being is *always* wrong; that courage is *always* a virtue? In other words, does truth, moral or otherwise, change with society, popular opinion, experimental testing – or is it absolute and unchanging?

One possible way to examine this question is to consider an illustration that defines the absolutist perspective (there is universal Truth that does not change) and the relativistic point of view (all truth is subject to change). A father sits his five-year old son down and begins to give him an *absolutist* lecture on lying. He begins, "Johnny, I don't want you ever to tell a lie. Never, ever lie. I don't care what the situation is or how much trouble you might get into – it is wrong to lie." Now, with the same scenario in mind, a father gives a *relativistic* discourse on lying. He commences, "Johnny, lying is wrong. I do not want you to tell lies, except if you feel you have no other choice. You should not lie unless you absolutely feel like you have too."

In Peter Kreeft's insightful work, *A Refutation of Moral Relativism*, the validity of absolute truth versus relativistic thought is debated via a series of conversations. Kreeft, who is Professor of Philosophy at Boston College, begins by defining moral relativism as that which denies an absolute law for man; instead, insisting that *good* and *evil* are man-made.[25] The modern day translation of that sentiment goes something like, "Whatever you think is true for you is ok, and whatever I think works for me is also ok." He goes on to say that relativism is the philosophy that denies absolutes – any absolutes. Professor Kreeft asserts that everyone believes there are many relativities – that some things are relative – but relativism claims that *all* things are relative.[26] In other words, relativism is the idea that all propositions are morally equal and, therefore, there is no binding objective (or absolute) truth. Modern day translation: "There is no *one* right answer."

Having defined the position of relativism, Kreeft then turns to absolutism as that which is not transitional but, rather, necessary. He continues, "Absolutes are universal and objective and have three characteristics that distinguish them. An absolute truth is not relative to time, so it does not change. It is not relative to place or nation or class or culture or race or gender or any group – it is universal. Third, (absolute truth) is not relative to opinion or thought or belief or desire or feeling or any subjective consciousness. It is objectively real, objectively true, whether I or you or anyone else knows it, or believes it, or likes it, or cares about it."[27] In this sense, absolute or universal *Truth* is eternal both in origin and in content – meaning *Truth* has always existed in time and is beyond societal fads or personal opinions. Again quoting Fernandez-

---

[25] Peter Kreeft, *A Refutation of Moral Relativism* (San Francisco, Ignatius Press, 1999), 23.
[26] Peter Kreeft, *A Refutation of Moral Relativism* (San Francisco, Ignatius Press, 1999), 28.
[27] Peter Kreeft, *A Refutation of Moral Relativism* (San Francisco, Ignatius Press, 1999), 30.

Armesto, "When we speak of truth as eternal, we mean something other than the property of a sentence or proposition: we mean reality itself – the truth which must be eternal because falsehood or nothingness could not precede it; the absolute truth which is the ultimate object of every search for truth."[28]

Of course, these definitions are nothing new or novel in the history of philosophical thought. One can return to the ancient Sophists of Plato's day and listen to their most famous teacher Protagoras proclaim that "man is the measure of all things." In other words, man decides what is good, bad, true, and so on. The concept that "man is the measure of all things" declares that anything virtuous or vile – true or false – is understandable only in relation to individual opinion. Consequently, all any person can *know* is what one learns from one's culture, conditioning, and experience. Thus, Protagoras's doctrine of relativism asserts that knowledge is meaningful, not in some ultimate sense, but (only) in how it *affects* us.[29]

Some took and furthered this mentality into solipsism – the view that the self alone exists as the source of all knowledge; while others like the Epicureans submersed themselves into materialism and hedonism. Whatever the diversion, followers of relativism look to *themselves* for answers, definitions, and purpose. They believe man is both the cause and cure for all of humanity's problems. This had led many relativists to intimate encounters with despair, anxiety, dread, and confusion – not unlike, according to Peter Kreeft, the story of two men shipwrecked on an island who find a message one day floating in a bottle. Ferociously they tear the paper out of the bottle and

---

[28] Felipe Fernandez-Armesto, *Truth, A History and a Guide for the Perplexed* (New York, Thomas Dunne, 1997), 26.
[29] Joan A. Price, *Philosophy Through the Ages* (Belmont, Wadsworth, 2000), 26.

read it with hopeful anticipation for answers from an outside, ultimate source – only to discover that the message is one *they* themselves sent out weeks before. As philosophy professor Dr. Gerard Reed so eloquently deduces, "Deafened by our own sounds, we easily imagine we're the source of all that is."[30]

The sheer folly of relativistic thinking lies in the inherit contradiction within the very definition. Simply stated, relativism proclaims, "There are no absolute truths." One need not look long to see the crack that lies at the base of this formula. The statement – by the way, this tenet is the bedrock of relativism – cannot sustain itself. "There are no absolute truths" should correctly be translated to read, "There are no absolute truths, except for <u>this absolute truth</u> that says, there are no absolute truths." In other words, the statement, "There are no absolute truths" is itself, an absolute statement or truth. It is very much like trying to say with a straight face, "The *truth* is that there is no *truth*." Thus, the very heart and soul of relativism falls under its own weight of critical examination.

Without absolutism, or without an absolute (universal) standard that is not subject to change, the relativist could not even make the claim, "There are no absolutes." Trying to have an argument about any topic without a standard from which to judge is much like having a race in which the finish line (the standard) is constantly moving. How will anyone know who won? How will the runners know when to stop? Who proclaims that the race is officially over? As C. S. Lewis has commented, "The moment you say that one set of moral ideas can be better than another, you are in fact, measuring them both by a *standard*, saying that one of them conforms to that (absolute) standard more nearly than the other...(also) the standard that

---

[30] Gerard Reed, *C. S. Lewis Explores Vice and Virtue* (Kansas City, Beacon Hill Press, 2001), 99.

measures two things is something *different* from either."[31] If man is left to himself to define good, evil, right, wrong, truth, and falsehood as he individually sees fit – without any standard – then how is man ever to know what, if any, of the definitions are correct? Who has the authority to say *this* opinion is true but *that* opinion or act is wrong. Indeed, under relativistic conditions, a society can never fully say a definition is "correct," "good," "bad," or even "wrong" because that would imply an absolute standard from which one is measuring against. Thus, even in trying to *prove* relativism as a valid option, one must intrinsically admit to some sort of universal or absolute criteria.

---

[31] Armand M. Nicholi, *The Question of God* (New York, The Free Press, 2002), 62.

Chapter Three

*- I went to the woods because I wanted to live
deliberately...I wanted to live deep and suck out all the
marrow of life! To put to rout all that was not life...And
not, when I came to die, discover that I had not lived...*

- Thoreau

One may ask what all this talk of universal or
relativistic philosophy has to do with existential thought.
Succinctly stated, since existentialism is about
questioning who we are and why we exist, it is
essential to know whether our answers are mere
subjective opinion or if they have any attachment to
universal truth. To that end, the Socratic dictum, "The
unexamined life is not worth living" serves as the heart
and soul of all existential inquiry.

For centuries, the human heart has been
plagued with questions that center on the idea of
individual meaning. "Why do I exist?" "Is their
universal Truth?" "Can I know what is right and
wrong?" "Is there a God or afterlife?" "Why is there
suffering?" Perhaps Martin Heidegger summed up all
of these questions most courageously when he asked,
"Why is there something rather than nothing?"

For most people, these questions receive little
philosophical scrutiny and analysis; however, the
existentialist fully embraces these dilemmas as the
foundation of his existence. As he endeavors to "think
through" his own personal beliefs and positions on
significant moral issues, the existential thinker displays
the importance of a life lived in the pursuit of a greater
degree of philosophical awareness. The ongoing
assumption, which drives this incessant hunger for

individual authenticity, is that neutrality in one's personal philosophy is neither possible nor desirable. In this sense, it is important to remember that all individuals *are* philosophers because all will have to form an opinion (philosophy) regarding life's deep and troubling questions. This philosophic journey into truthfulness, or what Kierkegaard called "the challenge of being human," delivers the sincere seeker from superficial explanations that often falsely patronize the modern mind and spirit. Furthermore, existential reflection requires – nay, demands – consistent internal examination of one's actions and motives, thus providing one with a vision of what a genuine and authentic existence can and should be. In the end, though not often easy or comfortable, this type of self-evaluation – existential existence – is far more profound and beneficial than the shallow solutions offered today by modern "pop" psychology and talk show hosts.

Yet, perhaps one of the most penetrating lessons a person will learn from living in an existential (self-evaluating) manner is the following maxim: *never* try to "get the answer" to a philosophical dilemma before understanding *all* the pertinent questions. As Phillip Johnson, who taught law for over thirty years at the University of California, Berkeley wrote, "The best way to approach a problem of any kind is usually not to talk or even think very much about the ultimate answer until one has made sure that one is asking all the right questions in the right order. When I am too eager to get to the answer, I may overlook some of the preliminary questions because I do not stop to reflect on why they are important and assume carelessly that I must already have answered them."[32] Thus, only after asking the pertinent and necessary questions

---

[32] Phillip Johnson, *The Right Questions* (Downers Grove, InterVarsity Press, 2002), 27.

concerning a given topic is one, existentially speaking, ready to formulate an educated and sincere reply. Ultimately, what humanity will discover, living in a state of inner contemplation, is the realization of the vast depths that lie within us, and of the daring and determination it takes to explore them in order to become all that a human being can and should be.[33]

In continuing to evaluate existential principles, it should be noted that the field of existentialism can be divided into two major spheres: religious and secular. Both schools are fundamentally concerned with individual existence and choice; however, each system of thought arrives at a very different conclusion regarding ultimate meaning. Briefly stated, secular or non-religious existential authors thoroughly define man "as the measure of all things" with little or no possibility of universal meaning or purpose. This interpretation is captured succinctly by playwright Albert Camus who, in his novel *The Plague*, has a main character state, "I have no idea what's awaiting me, or what will happen when all this ends."[34] On the other hand, non-secular or religious existential thinkers tend to tie man's individual existence and function with a Divine element – the Creator has made a meaningful world that has definite order and purpose. This view is summarized pointedly by philosopher Francis Schaeffer in his work, *Death in the City*, where he asserts, "For man is not just a chance configuration of atoms in the slipstream of meaningless chance history. No. Man, made in the image of God, has a purpose – to be in relationship to the God who is there. And whether it is in Jeremiah's day, or in our own recent generations, the effect is the

---

[33] John Mullen, *Kierkegaard's Philosophy: Self-Deception and Cowardice in the Present Age* (New York, Meridian, 1981), Preface.

[34] Colin Chapman, *The Case for Christianity* (Grand Rapids, Eerdmans, 1981), 216.

same. Man forgets his purpose, and thus he forgets who he is and what life means."[35]

Turning to a closer examination of secular existentialism, one discovers six common themes or principles usually associated with this division of existential thought. The first theme is predicated upon the idea that 'existence precedes essence' or the importance of the individual over labels. Contrary to the medieval notion that all life had inherit design and meaning even *before* existence (birth), secular existentialism taught that life only *receives* meaning *after* one exists and creates his own value. According to Jean-Paul Sartre, "This is the first principle of existentialism because it states that man *first* exists and *then* defines (or gives meaning to) his existence. This means, according to Sartre and other secular existentialists, that life has no meaning in and of itself (in or out of the womb) – only the significance or value that each individual chooses to give it. An individual's life has no ultimate meaning, in any grand or universal sense, unless – or until – that person decides to give his life meaning. Thus, since existence takes priority over essence, there can be no universal moral absolutes of right and wrong apart from what each individual opines appropriate.

The second theme is that of anxiety, anguish, fear and dread as the underlying condition of all human existence. Key to this thesis is the belief of 'nothingness' as it pertains to the condition of man and his destiny. Since one's existence is tied to emptiness and insignificance, it is only natural, according to the secular existentialist that one would despair over one's predicament in the universe. As the brilliant Russian author Dostoevsky once wrote, "If God (or absolute

---

[35] Francis Schaeffer, *The Complete Works of Francis Schaeffer, Volume Four* (Wheaton, Crossway Books, 1982), 214.

Truth) does not exist, then everything is permitted."[36] The secular existentialist, completely missing Dostoevsky's point, insists that since there is no God (or absolute Truth), everything is indeed permitted...and man is in consequence forlorn (abandoned), for he cannot find anything to depend upon either within or outside himself.[37] Whereas Dostoevsky was making this point to emphasize the necessity of there being a God (absolute Truth), the atheist Sartre used (the point) to make clear the implications of atheism. For Sartre (and the secular existentialist), because there is no God, there is no realm of values and moral rules apart from us that we can use to guide our lives...morality is (thus) not discovered; it is chosen or invented by each individual, much like creating a work of art.[38]

The third and fourth themes are that of absurdity and existence as nothingness or void, meaning that life is inexplicable and without infinite value or structure. In Sartre's novel, *Nausea*, individual existence is portrayed as inconsequential and ultimately meaningless. Sartre writes, "I was just thinking...that here we are, all of us, eating and drinking, to preserve our precious existence, and that there's nothing, nothing, absolutely no reason for existing."[39] Further emphasizing this point, Sartre, in *Existentialism and Human Emotions*, writes, "If God does not exist, we find no values or commands to turn to which legitimize our conduct. So, in the bright realm of values, we have no excuse behind us, nor justification before us. We

---

[36] Colin Chapman, *The Case for Christianity* (Grand Rapids, Eerdmans, 1981), 213.

[37] Colin Chapman, *The Case for Christianity* (Grand Rapids, Eerdmans, 1981), 213.

[38] William Lawhead, *The Philosophical Journey* (Mountain View, Mayfield Publishing, 2000), 531.

[39] Colin Chapman, *The Case for Christianity* (Grand Rapids, Eerdmans, 1981), 211.

are alone, with no excuses...To say that we invent values means nothing else but this: life has no meaning 'a priori'."[40]

The fifth and six themes are death and the alienation of the individual. Again, one can turn to Sartre to capture the essence of these ideas. As the secular existentialist summed up, "Death is the total wiping out of my existence as a conscious being and therefore is another witness to the absurdity of humanity." Sartre continues, "Man will do nothing unless he has first understood that he must count on no one but himself; that he is alone, abandoned on earth in the midst of his infinite responsibilities; without help, with no other aim than the one he sets himself, with no other destiny than the one he forges for himself on this earth."[41]

Another non-religious (secular) existential writer, Albert Camus, proclaimed that "death is philosophy's only problem" worthy of investigation. Like Sartre, Camus was fixated on man's inevitable appointment with death and the preposterousness of having to live while awaiting that event. Camus' noted work, *Myth of Sisyphus*, portrays man attempting to measure the nature and meaning of an essentially meaningless and absurd universe. The mythological Sisyphus, eternally pushing a huge rock uphill, only to have it roll to the bottom again, typifies (for the secular existentialist) the human condition. He finds no ultimate value or point in his struggle, yet he will continue on with "silent joy."[42]

In stark contrast, the religious school of existential thought sees a direct correlation between individual meaning and the existence of universal truth.

---

[40] Jean-Paul Sartre, *Existentialism and Human Emotions* (New York, Philosophical Library, 1957), 23,49.
[41] Manuel Velasquez, *Philosophy* (Belmont, Wadsworth, 2002), 98.
[42] Norman Geisler and Paul Feinberg, *Introduction to Philosophy* (Grand Rapids, Baker Books, 1980), 93.

As opposed to viewing life as absurd or pointless, the religious existentialist beholds man as a work of wonder, with purpose, potential, and ultimate meaning. Within this school of philosophical thought, one is drawn immediately to the writings of the "father of existentialism" Soren Kierkegaard. As with all existential writers, Kierkegaard calls on one to live a life of self-examination and authenticity. Yet, unlike Camus or Sartre, Kierkegaard seems sure that life has ultimate meaning and design. Because he is so confident of this, he diligently urges his readers to pursue a life of examination that will lead one to finding his true – essential – self. In his work, *The Sickness Unto Death*, Kierkegaard stated, "The biggest danger, that of losing oneself (not discovering who one is or why one exists), can pass off in the world as quietly as if it were nothing; every other loss, an arm, a leg, five dollars, a wife, is bound to be noticed."[43]

For Kierkegaard, human life receives meaning and value from the source of creation itself and not from the "raging elements" confronting a person. Far from an individual having to create his own significance, religious existentialism teaches that each person possess meaning inherently. What a person does with this possibility of living a "full existence" does not depend upon what he understands but, rather, upon what he wills. Life is, for the non-secular (or religious) existentialist, all about choices and decisions that cannot be isolated from one's habits and understanding of universal meaning. When studying religious existential thought, one is instantly reminded of Aristotle and the prime importance he placed on *individual* habits coinciding with *individual* virtue and meaning. Indeed, Aristotle would magnificently capture

---

[43] Soren Kierkegaard, *The Sickness Unto Death* (London, Penguin Books, 1985), 62.

27

the essence of this notion with his oft-quoted phrase, "We are what we repeatedly do."

In *Fear and Trembling*, Kierkegaard echoes this sentiment and calls on individuals to understand the importance of evaluating their existence and motives. He pointedly asks, "How many people are there now with the passion to judge themselves honestly? The very thought of taking time on one's conscience, of giving conscience time to search out with its sleepless perseverance every secret thought... and call forth by anguish itself if by nothing else, the dark passions which after all lie concealed in every human life...yet such things worry people little in this age...How many nowadays understand what the absurd is...how many are even simply honest enough to know what they are...?"[44] Kierkegaard furthered his anthem of introspective awareness in yet another work, *Purity of Heart*, where he writes, "To exist religiously (or at the highest level of consciousness) is then to be reflective and transparent to oneself. This means among other things to put aside all 'busyness'...so that one has hours to collect his mind, so that his life can win transparency. 'Busyness' is not, of course, an accidental impediment to transparency, (being authentic), but rather a tactic to avoid it."[45] In his recent work, *Civility: Manners, Morals, and the Etiquette of Democracy*, Yale Law School professor Stephen Carter corroborates Kierkegaard's thoughts and suggests that modern man is too busy, too addicted to clocks and calendars, too immersed in noise, to discern truths. He warns, "If we lose the vast silences that help define the

---

[44] Soren Kierkeegard, *Fear and Trembling* (London, Penguin Books, 1985), 126-127.
[45] John Mullen, *Kierkegaard's Philosophy: Self-Deception and Cowardice in the Present Age* (New York, Meridian, 1981), 142.

sounds that fall between them, we may lose the ability to appreciate the transcendent."[46]

One may also look to other resources besides Soren Kierkegaard to find a treasure of religious or non-secular existential analysis. For example, one can turn to the acclaimed author Herman Melville, who points out in chapter ninety-seven of *Moby Dick*, that "the greatest book of all books – Ecclesiastes" is an existential masterpiece. Similarly, in the same category of classic religious existential texts, one can study Pascal's *Pensees*, Aquinas' *Summa Theologica*, or Dostoevsky's *Brother Karamazov*, to appreciate more fully the vast difference between the secular and religious existential points of view.

Perhaps no writer does this more simply and succinctly than the Oxford scholar C. S. Lewis who uses the metaphor of ships to illustrate the significance of religious existentialism. According to Lewis, the first question that ethics – indeed all of existential philosophy – must address is, "How can my ship (my life) exist with other ships?" The area of social ethics, or co-existing with our fellow human beings (other ships), plays an enormous role in understanding what our individual and collective purpose is. Lewis goes on to discuss the second most important question, "How can my ship (my life) avoid decay?" Again, the area of individual ethics is paramount if one is going to avoid self-destruction – or worse – living a life that is not authentic. Finally, the third question to ponder, according to Lewis, is "What is my ship's (my life's) ultimate mission or destiny?" C. S. Lewis suggests that ships need to know both why they are being set out to sea and where their final destination will be. Similarly, individual human beings must seek with all their might

---

[46] Gerard Reed, *C. S. Lewis Explores Vice and Virtue* (Kansas City, Beacon Hill Press, 2001), 99.

to understand both why they exist and where they are going.

In his classic work, *The Will to Believe*, William James showed that any adequate philosophy must satisfy two kinds of human distress. One is theoretical, or the intellectual concern to form a general conception of the universe; the second is practical, or the moral and religious desire to include man's passionate natures in any philosophical consideration of how men are to act and what they should believe.[47] Herman Dooyerweerd, a Dutch professor of philosophy, makes an analogous point saying, "Ultimately, the problem of the meaning of history revolves around the question: 'Who is man himself and what is his origin and final destination'?"[48] The student of existentialism – whether secular or religious – echoes these sentiments by quoting the wisdom of an ancient Roman Stoic. According to the philosopher Seneca, "If one would enjoy freedom, one must be a slave to philosophy because the body once cured, often ails again, but the mind (soul) once cured is healed for good." Indeed, it is precisely the discipline of existential thought that provides such a remedy for man by compelling him to examine personal beliefs and ideas. This is not to say that other schools of philosophy do not lend the reader to self-examination. However, writers of existential philosophy, whether in literature, poetry, movies, or songs, are distinctly more effective and adept in causing the reader to ponder his or her own destiny and role in the universe.

---

[47] Frank Magill, *Masterpieces of World Philosophy* (New York, Harper Collins, 1990), 445.
[48] Coin Chapman, *The Case for Christianity* (Grand Rapids, Eerdmans, 1981), 67.

Chapter Four

- Many people fear nothing more terribly than to take a position which stands out sharply and clearly from prevailing opinion. The tendency of most is to adopt a view that is so ambiguous that it will include everything, and so popular that it will include everyone.

- Martin Luther King, Jr.

While I am convinced that all philosophers are existentialists to one degree or another, this work will primarily focus on four significant thinkers: Soren Kierkegaard (1813-1855), Friedrich Nietzsche (1844-1900), Jean-Paul Sartre (1905-1980), and C. S. Lewis (1898-1963). These reflective thinkers represent the depth and vastness of the school of existentialism through their works and individual lives. Through their words, we can fully explore the core concerns of philosophy – namely, truth, meaning, existence, suffering, and death.

Soren Kierkegaard, sometimes referred to as the "Danish Socrates," was born in Copenhagen, Denmark and was the youngest of seven children. Much has been written about Kierkegaard's relationship with his oppressive father who was a devout Lutheran racked with guilt over certain moral failures. Perhaps the intensely strict environment that Soren grew up in caused the youthful Kierkegaard to exchange his academic studies in theology for a more carefree existence of drinking and partying. Yet, no matter how boisterous and popular Kierkegaard was at social outings, inwardly he could never escape the shame, guilt, and despair that was so familiar to his father. We have a glimpse into this despondency from an entry in *The Journals*, which record the following selection: "I have just returned from a party of which I was the life and soul; wit poured from my lips, everyone laughed and admired me but I went away...and wanted to shoot myself."[49] This seemingly "double-life" existence of smiling on the outside while crying with loneliness on the inside, is something that many, in any period of history, can relate too. Indeed, many would argue that it is specifically because of this epoch in Kierkegaard's life that his later writings on being authentic and living above the level of superficiality have legitimacy.

Whatever the case, Kierkegaard's troubles were by no means over even after he reconciled with his father and with his own personal demons of indiscriminant carousing. Another major source of contention within the life of Kierkegaard was his relationship and engagement with Regina Olsen. Though passionately in love with the much younger Regina, Kierkegaard, then twenty-seven, agonized over their courtship as he worried that his despondent personality would eventually undermine any chance of a happy union. It is during this period that the existentialist in Kierkegaard comes to fruition as he realizes that cold logic and distant theories cannot solve his dilemma with Regina. He is compelled, all alone, to make a subjective decision that will undeniably alter the rest of his existence. He chooses to break off the engagement and live the rest of his life with all of the consequences associated with that all-important decision. With absolute Spartan-like focus, Kierkegaard decides that he must "live a life wholly dedicated to God" with no distractions – including energies spent on or with Regina. It was an existential moment, to say the least, in that the ramifications of

---

[49] Soren Kierkegaard, *The Journals of Kierkegaard* (London, Collins, 1958), 54.

this single decision magnified the overall importance of the individual self. Though critics point out, and perhaps rightly so, that Kierkegaard could have been "wholly" dedicated to both God and wife, Kierkegaard was, nonetheless, on his way to becoming the chief expositor of existential theory.

With his famous "truth as subjectivity" proclamation, Kierkegaard sought to define authentic existence as the passing from one "stage of life" to another. Promising that these intervals always involve periods of anxiety, Kierkegaard sought to challenge Friedrich Hegel's emphasis of a necessary or predetermined existence and replace it with a more radical focus on individual decision. In his work, *Philosophical Fragments*, published in 1844, Kierkegaard urged his readers to study his "three stages of life" formula so that they could better comprehend who they were and, perhaps more importantly, to know where they were on the journey towards self-actualization.

The first stage, commonly referred to as the 'aesthetic' level, is one where individuals seek freedom from boredom. In this stage, a person is primarily concerned with only selfish pleasures or outer, superficial beauty. The search for universal Truth or absolutes, much less individual meaning, is virtually non-existent at this echelon. Even a cursory evaluation of mankind's current state of affairs causes one to wonder if our present hunger for superficial pleasures and toys is not exactly what Kierkegaard was writing about.

The next stage, the 'ethical' level, is one in which the individual begins to accept obligations, commitments, rules and authority. No longer pleased with fading gratification, this person begins to search for his essential self. This individual is driven by a sense of duty, not unlike Immanuel Kant's "ought implies must" imperative. According to author John

Mullen, it is not up to the individual to decide *what* his place in the universe is at this level. Rather, it is up to the individual at this stage to decide *if* he will take his place in the universe. If he accepts his place, his life task is just beginning, namely to develop this ethically planned self. Thus, man's freedom, that which distinguishes him from all else, lies not in deciding who he is to be, or in creating a place for himself in existence, it lies rather in the ability to accept (or not) one's place, and carry out (or not) the duties assigned to it.[50]

Finally, the third stage, or the 'religious' level, is one of complete self-actualization where the individual sees himself as a creature dependent upon God for existence and ultimate meaning. Again, in *Fear and Trembling*, Kierkegaard illustrates the basic yet profound difference between the ethical stage and the comprehensive religious stage. By focusing on the example of Abraham and his willingness to sacrifice his son out of obedience to God's request, Kierkegaard shows how the religious stage may require an individual to suspend his ethical concerns. This "teleological suspension of the ethical" points out that one's duty is neither personal nor social – it exists out of a sense of obedience to God.

Continuing with the theme of individual choice, Kierkegaard also took issue with Hegel's definition of truth. Hegel thought of truth as the synthesis of opposing viewpoints where nothing is true in any *absolute* sense. All that man can expect, argued Hegel, is that one idea (thesis) will be challenged by an opposite idea (antithesis), and that this will in turn be superseded by an idea which transcends the two

---

[50] John Mullen, *Kierkegaard's Philosophy: Self-Deception and Cowardice in the Present Age* (New York, Meridian, 1981), 124.

34

contradictory ideas (synthesis).[51] In other words, there can be no absolute or universal Truth because Truth is continually unfolding in each and every situation and generation. Kierkegaard, on the other hand, openly embraced absolute Truth but placed greater emphasis on interaction as opposed to mere mental assent. He viewed absolute or universal truth as a basis or aid that allowed one to make the principles of Truth applicable to one's life.

Although Kierkegaard cautioned against the possibility of universal truth becoming a distraction, he nonetheless saw absolute (universal) truth as a necessary foundation. Not that Kierkegaard was against absolutes; rather, he simply tried to inform his audience that there was no substitute for individual choice and personal accountability. While not denying the existence of objective scientific truth, Kierkegaard simply *did* not consider that kind of truth important, at least not nearly as important as subjective truth.[52] It is here that the reader of Kierkegaard must be careful. When Kierkegaard speaks of the importance of 'subjective truth', he is *not* espousing a purely relativistic approach to philosophy. Indeed, Kierkegaard's "truth is subjectivity" theme does not mean that any subjective belief is to be considered true. Rather, all Kierkegaard means by his "truth as subjectivity" thesis is that unless one believes something *subjectively* – inwardly and passionately – he does not possess the truth at all. Truth is always personal and not merely propositional.[53]

Kierkegaard stated that there was no point in asking, "What is the truth?" because it is impossible, he

---

[51] Colin Chapman, *The Case for Christianity* (Grand Rapids, Eerdmans, 1981), 168.

[52] Norman Geisler and Paul Feinberg, *Introduction to Philosophy* (Grand Rapids, Baker Books, 1980), 46.

[53] Norman Geisler and Paul Feinberg, *Introduction to Philosophy* (Grand Rapids, Baker Books, 1980), 46.

believed, to know the truth objectively or impartially. The question we must ask, he insisted, is "What is the truth for me and how am I to live my life?"[54] In other words, Kierkegaard, far from espousing that each individual creates different and personal versions of truth, is demanding that one's actions correspond or reflect one's understanding of truth. Kierkegaard is far more concerned with "being true" than simply knowing "what is true." The difference, for Kierkegaard, is between knowing the truth as something out there external to me and living (that) truth as something that affects every aspect of my life. For example, a person could intellectually embrace a very elevated moral theory but be a scoundrel in actual practice. Such a person would *objectively* know the truth but would not be *subjectively* living in that truth.[55]

Leo Tolstoy's story *The Death of Ivan Illych* concretely illustrates the difference between knowing the truth intellectually and knowing it subjectively – personally, inwardly, and passionately. Ivan Illych had always known the (absolute or universal) truth of the statement, "all men are mortal." But "men" in that statement was abstract (not personal). Ivan could not envision it as including him. One day at his doctor's office, however, Ivan discovered that *he* was dying. Suddenly, the objective truth he had always known took on a new meaning. The inevitability of death was easy to contemplate when it referred to humanity in general. But when Ivan realized that "I, Ivan Illych, am dying," the concept of mortality suddenly changed him.[56]

---

[54] Colin Chapman, *The Case for Christianity* (Grand Rapids, Eerdmans, 1981), 169.
[55] William Lawhead, *The Philosophical Journey* (Mountain View, Mayfield Publishing, 2000), 186.
[56] William Lawhead, *The Philosophical Journey* (Mountain View, Mayfield Publishing, 2000), 188.

For Kierkegaard, reality cannot be separated from existence because to exist means to make decisions, not to flounder.[57] For Kierkegaard, it is impossible to be a voyeur if one is trying to live an authentic existential existence. One hardly gains truth by mere observation, but by obedience; never by being a spectator, but only by being a participator in life. Truth is found in the concrete, not in the abstract; in the existential, not in the rational.[58] Thus, for Kierkegaard, "truth is subjectivity" is not a pathetic version of the "what's true for me" syndrome, but instead *is the highest* truth that an "existing individual" can arrive at.

To this end, Kierkegaard found that it was not the objective philosopher but the authentic individualist who put forth the greatest amount of effort in examining matters of truth and transparent living. Human beings, he said, are not objective spectators, but actors involved in the drama of existence. The truly existing individual must be passionate as well as conscious.[59] In *Concluding Unscientific Postscript*, Kierkegaard writes, It is impossible to exist without passion, unless we understand the word "exist" in the loose sense of a so-called existence. Every Greek thinker was therefore essentially a passionate thinker." He accentuated this point in an ingenious way through his writings – or style of writing. Kierkegaard used several different devices to rouse the reader's emotion and went so far as to undermine even his own authority as an author. By using pseudonyms in many different ways, Kierkegaard deflected the responsibility for understanding his writings from himself (the author) to the shoulders of his readers. In this way, Kierkegaard, much like

---

[57] Manuel Velasquez, *Philosophy* (Belmont, Wadsworth, 2002), 225.
[58] Norman Geisler and Paul Feinberg, *Introduction to Philosophy* (Grand Rapids, Baker Books, 1980), 46.
[59] Joan A. Price, *Philosophy Through the Ages* (Belmont, Wadsworth, 2000), 314.

Socrates with his use of dialectic exchange, places the onus of action and response squarely on the individual in question. As a result, though his writings represented a wide variety of styles and specific topics, they were all directed to calling individuals to live authentic, passionate, and honest lives, repudiating the temptation to find our meaning and identity in institutions or abstractions.[60]

It is well documented that Soren Kierkegaard thought very little of crowds, groups or organizations. Seen as contraptions bent on destroying one's individuality and uniqueness, Kierkegaard did not hesitate to attack these gatherings. No clique or club – sacred or secular – was beyond his criticism. In fact, despite being regarded as a chief spokesman for religious existentialism, Kierkegaard spoke out most notably against the organized church of his day. Yet, when he viciously attacked Christianity, he did so in the defense of "becoming a Christian."[61] Kierkegaard's primary problem was with the entity of Christendom and not with an individual coming to and living out the Christian faith. In fact, Kierkegaard wanted his readers to visualize the understanding that humanity, as a collective whole did not exist, *only* individual human beings. Moreover, it is these individual persons who must undergo an "annihilation process" by which they put themselves out of the way in order to truly find God.[62] Kierkegaard further writes, "To exist religiously is to be reflective and transparent to oneself; putting

[60] William Lawhead, *The Philosophical Journey* (Mountain View, Mayfield, 2000), 185.

[61] Robert Solomon, *From Hegel to Existentialism* (New York, Oxford University Press, 1987), 72.

[62] John Mullen, *Kierkegaard's Philosophy: Self-Deception and Cowardice in the Present Age* (New York, Meridian, 1981), 139.

aside all busyness so that one has hours to collect his mind and win transparency."[63]

With his tremendous emphasis on personal involvement in existential decisions, Kierkegaard saw as sheer folly the common practice of claiming a sacred right due to birth. Protesting against the idea that one was "automatically" a 'Christian' simply because one was born into a 'Christian' family or country, Kierkegaard sought to re-define religious conversion. One needed to choose – willfully – to make a religious decision for it to have any existential significance. Perhaps this is why Kierkegaard chose the extreme example of Abraham to illustrate his point on active participation in one's convictions. According to Genesis, God requires Abraham to sacrifice his son at the top of a mountain. Though God eventually intervenes and spares the child, Abraham is willing to sacrifice his son in order to be counted as a true follower – in other words, Abraham needed to *act* upon his beliefs.

Several decades earlier, the brilliant French thinker Blaise Pascal (1623-1662) contrived writings with very similar themes concerning individuality, personal faith, and the condition of man. Like Socrates, Pascal motivated his audience to examine their lives, actions, and motives in the context of finding ultimate meaning. Pascal, like the later Kierkegaard, placed great emphasis on the *individual* examining his own *individual* existence. In particular, Pascal noted with dismay how man seemed content with distracting himself from the most critical aspect of being fully human – that of self-examination. As Pascal wrote, "Perhaps we distract ourselves because looking at our lives confronts us with our lack of meaning, our unhappiness, and our loneliness – and with the

---

[63] John Mullen, *Kierkegaard's Philosophy: Self-Deception and Cowardice in the Present Age* (New York, Meridian, 1981), 142.

difficulty, the fragility, and the unbelievable brevity of life"[64]

Kierkegaard, mirroring the thoughts of Pascal, continually emphasized in his writings the importance of habitual self-examination. He insisted that true faith – as well as truthful existence – was centered with one's will and not with one's intellect. He accentuated this conviction by saying, "Becoming a Christian has nothing to do with a change in the intellect, but in the will. This change is the most painful of all operations, comparable to vivisection (dismemberment)." This is precisely why Kierkegaard referred to the process of becoming a Christian as taking a "leap of faith" because when a person takes this chance (conversion), "he lives entirely full of the idea of risking his life for it: and his life is the proof that he believes."[65]

Kierkegaard believed that for such an individual, sincere and passionate religious faith stood as the principle reason one is able to become one's true, transparent self. Kierkegaard captured the essence of this type of active belief when he recorded in his *Journals*, "What I really lack is to be clear in my mind *what I am to do*, not what I am to know, except in so far as certain understanding must precede every action. The thing is to understand myself, to see what God really wishes me to do; the thing is to find a truth which is true for me, to find *the idea for which I can live and die.* Kierkegaard continued, "What would be the use of discovering so-called objective truth, of working through all the systems of philosophy and of being able, if required, to review them all and show up the inconsistencies within each system; - what good would it do me to be able to explain the meaning of

---

[64] Armand M. Nicholi, *The Question of God* (New York, The Free Press, 2002), 6.
[65] Colin Chapman, *The Case for Christianity* (Grand Rapids, Eerdmans, 1981), 170.

40

Christianity if it had no deeper significance *for me and my life...?*[66]

In *Concluding Unscientific Postscript*, Soren Kierkegaard wrote that genuine existence meant that one was always to be in the process of becoming. This is to say that a religious existentialist is perpetually examining his convictions, motives and lifestyle – in all areas of his life – to ensure genuine and sincere existence. In terms of a specifically *religious* existence, Kierkegaard called this becoming *transparent* before oneself and one's Creator. The choice of faith, then, is more an activity of the will than of the intellect – not made as a "once for all" sales-type business transaction. Rather, the individual person who decides to believe religiously and participate in faith must continually renew his commitment day by day. Kierkegaard declared that true faith must be existential because it depends entirely on the choice of the will. He writes, "From the Christian point of view, faith belongs to the existential because God did not appear in the character of a professor who has some doctrines which must first be believed and then understood. No, faith belongs to and has its home in the existential, and in all eternity it has nothing to do with knowledge as a comparative or a superlative."[67]

Thus, without the process of habitual and intense subjectivity – making one's beliefs part of one's actual life – Kierkegaard warned that even the religious individual would simply become part of the indifferent masses. By not making faith a living part of his activities, the disingenuous individual merely "will be forever running errands in life" and thus become bored with his religion and superficial faith. The sincere

---

[66] Soren Kierkegaard, *The Journals of Kierkegaard* (London, Collins, 1958), 4.

[67] Colin Chapman, *The Case for Christianity* (Grand Rapids, Eerdmans, 1981), 170.

religious existentialist, on the other hand, soon discovers that one is truly religious in direct proportion to the degree of his inward resignation, suffering, and consciousness of total indebtedness to the eternal.[68] Accordingly, Kierkegaard fittingly concludes that, "Disillusionment, melancholy, guilt, and ultimately despair await the individual who does not utilize (genuine) faith to escape alienated consciousness."

Toward the end of his life, Soren Kierkegaard waxed prophetic stating, "Not just in commerce but in the world of ideas too our age is putting on a veritable clearance sale. Everything can be had so dirt cheap that one begins to wonder whether in the end anyone will want to make a bid."[69] For Kierkegaard, there was absolutely one idea worth bidding on and preserving – that human life receives its meaning and value from the source of creation itself, (and) not from the raging elements and forces of creation that confront a person.[70] To that end, Kierkegaard argued in, *The Sickness Unto Death*, that the lowest form of offense was to leave the whole issue of religion undecided – in particular the whole issue of Christ. He fervently believed that once Christianity was presented to an individual, an existential choice had to be made. In other words, intellectual awareness about the Incarnate made it obligatory and imperative for that person to "make up his mind about Christ" because it was "an offense to be neutral about Him." As C. S. Lewis would suggest almost one hundred years later, vagueness about the person of Christ is impossible – either he was indeed God-man or he was a lunatic without equal. For Kierkegaard, Christ indeed was all that He proclaimed

---

[68] John Mullen, *Kierkegaard's Philosophy: Self-Deception and Cowardice in the Present Age* (New York, Meridian, 1981), 141.
[69] Soren Kierkegaard, *Fear and Trembling* (London, Penguin Books, 1985), 41.
[70] Soren Kierkegaard, *Fear and Trembling* (London, Penguin Books, 1985), 14.

to be – the "Absolute Paradox" that made it possible for the religious existentialist to live authentically and discover ultimate meaning.

Chapter Five

- Tomorrow, and tomorrow, and tomorrow, creeps in this petty pace from day to day to the last syllable of recorded time, and all our yesterdays have lighted fools, the way to dusty death. Out, out, brief candle! Life's but a walking shadow, a poor player that struts and frets his hour upon the stage and then is heard no more; it is a tale told by an idiot, full of sound and fury, signifying nothing.

- Macbeth

One could accurately say that what Soren Kierkegaard is to *religious* existential thought, Friedrich Nietzsche and Jean-Paul Sartre are too *non-religious* or secular existential thought.   Together, these two thinkers represent the side of existentialism that denies any essential human nature in the traditional sense, insisting that individuals create their own nature through free, responsible choices and actions.[71] Though these two men come from very different backgrounds and personal experiences, they each share the common secular existential view of *nihilism* – the summation that all is disordered and meaningless. With this sense of despair as a foundation of secular existentialism, perhaps there is no better place to begin our journey than with the theories of philosopher and author Friedrich Nietzsche.

Considered by many to be the "founder" of secular existentialism, Nietzsche's place in history has been summarized thus: "Widely rejected as a brilliant madman in the complacent atmosphere of pre-1914, a

---

[71] Manuel Velasquez, *Philosophy* (Belmont, Wadsworth, 2002), 96.

destructive and perverse genius who could not be taken really seriously, he stands today as the major prophet of the tortured twentieth century."[72] An intense atheist, Nietzsche left his boyhood faith behind during his twenties to pursue his interest in philology – the studying of ancient texts. Despite the fact that Nietzsche's grandfathers were devout Lutheran ministers, the college-aged Nietzsche seemed to find religious study continually less appealing. With his now famous, "That which does not kill me, only makes me stronger" mentality, Nietzsche found little use for the religious of the world who commiserated with the weak and feeble of society. In particular, Nietzsche had virtually no patience for Kierkegaard's brand of non-secular existentialism or religious expression. In his many works, Nietzsche openly displayed his utter contempt for the religious existentialist and, in particular, Christianity. He once wrote, "I regard Christianity as the most fatal and seductive lie that has ever yet existed...It seeks to keep life's failures – the defective, the diseased, the degenerating, the infirm, and the suffering – alive. Christianity contradicts nature when it asks us to love our enemies. By routing their thinking toward God, Christianity weakens the vital energies of the strong."[73]

Instead, Nietzsche began to become more enchanted with the writings of Arthur Schopenhauer who wrote about universal pessimism and, oddly enough, the wonders of music. The love of musical expression was particularly important to Nietzsche who, as a teenager, had composed piano and orchestral music. This interest in music also served as a foundation for Nietzsche's tumultuous friendship with

---

[72] William Lawhead, *The Voyage of Discovery, A Historical Introduction to Philosophy* (Belmont, Wadsworth, 2002), 416.
[73] Joan Price, *Philosophy Through the Ages* (Belmont, Wadsworth, 2000), 330.

the illustrious German composer Richard Wagner. Aside from their passion for music, both Wagner and Nietzsche held a common interest and admiration for the writings of Schopenhauer. As the impressionable Nietzsche immersed himself in Schopenhauer's *The World as Will and Representation*, and F. A. Lange's *History of Materialism and Critique of its Present Significance*, his prior religious convictions began to fade quickly. With his worldview and personal beliefs in a state of confusion, Nietzsche found himself leaving his Lutheran religious heritage for a newly embraced outlook that rejected any universal or absolute maxims.

While in his early twenties, Nietzsche began to fulfill his required military obligation serving in an equestrian field unit. After falling off a horse, Nietzsche suffered serious chest injuries and embarked on a journey of debilitating physical sufferings that would plague him throughout the rest of his life. In fact, just a few years later, his continued poor health became such an issue that he was forced to resign his teaching position from a Swiss university that he secured when he was a mere twenty-four years of age. From the time of his departure in 1878, until his death in 1900, Nietzsche spent the majority of his days in indescribable loneliness. Yet, despite serving as a professor at the University of Basel for only a few years, Nietzsche nonetheless distinguished himself as one of the foremost spokesmen for non-religious existentialism.

Born in 1844 in Roeken, Germany, Nietzsche lost his father while still a young boy. Much has been made of the fact that the young Nietzsche was subsequently raised by his mother, sister, aunts, and grandmother; however, whatever the effects, Nietzsche seemed to graduate adolescence as a bright young man, fully prepared for college studies. While a student at the University of Bonn, and then later at the University of Leipzig, Nietzsche began to embrace fully the teachings of Schopenhauer – specifically his attacks on Immanuel Kant's belief that reality is unknowable. Schopenhauer countered that reality can be, and is known to man as "Will" – or through our activities of individual choice and willing. The "Will" is the force behind all appearance and thus, it is the "Will" that is the *only* reality. Unfortunately for mankind, said Schopenhauer, the "Will" is full of self-conflict and so man's existence is ever plagued with continual discord and disillusionment – with no hope of ever finding any type of lasting satisfaction.

Nietzsche, intrigued with this newly found revelation, developed his own unique version of Schopenhauer's pessimistic and fatalistic philosophy. What eventually would come to be known as "perspectivism" – the rejection of traditional definitions of metaphysics and epistemology – grew out of one important question. Nietzsche boldly confronted the functionality of absolute truth by creating a system of philosophical thought that began with the following foundation: "Why truth? Why not rather untruth?" In his work, *The Will to Power*, (Section 552) Nietzsche argued that, "'Truth' is therefore not something there – that might be found or discovered – but something that must be created and that gives a name to a process, or rather to a will to overcome (but) that has in itself no end..." Nietzsche then went on to insist that individuals cannot know any reality beyond appearances, but added that these appearances are creatively structured by the subjective needs and values of each individual person. Thus, there is nothing absolute and everything is subjective.[74]

According to author William Lawhead, Nietzsche held that there could not be any uninterpreted "facts" or "truths" because everything we encounter is seen from

---

[74] William Lawhead, *The Voyage of Discovery, A Historical Introduction to Philosophy* (Belmont, Wadsworth, 2002), 348.

one perspective or another. In this way, Nietzsche stands as a paradigm case of a subjective relativist who states that the only reality we can know is the reality that is subjectively constructed by each individual.[75] Echoing Protagoras' "man is the measure of all things" ideology, Nietzsche even went so far as to deny the existence of facts as an objective standard for the truth. In his *Will to Power*, Nietzsche writes, "No, facts is precisely what there is not, only interpretations. We cannot establish any fact "in itself" – perhaps it is folly to want to do such a thing." Thus, by insisting that there are no "deeper" or "far above" (metaphysical) truths, Nietzsche announced that there is, therefore, no singular truth or truths about the universe – *except, of course, the truth that there is no singular truth about the universe.*

Assuming Nietzsche is correct that there is no objective universe to be known apart from one's perceptions, then one additional point must be addressed. If there is no objective truth, no standard apart from us by which our ideas may be measured, then it logically follows that there is no God – for if God existed, he would be an absolute standard of truth and value.[76] This conclusion laid the groundwork for Nietzsche's bold declaration that "God is dead" and that the Judeo-Christian influence on Western civilization was all but gone. In *The Gay Science*, Nietzsche wrote, "The greatest recent event – that "God is dead," that the belief in the Christian god has become unbelievable – is already beginning to cast its first shadows over Europe." Nietzsche proposed that the traditional values and ethical systems of the West were collapsing even as he wrote. The major source of

[75] William Lawhead, *The Philosophical Journey* (Mountain View, Mayfield, 2000), 191.
[76] William Lawhead, *The Philosophical Journey* (Mountain View, Mayfield, 2000), 197.

this collapse he felt, was the loss of belief in God. "God is dead," he declared, having been killed by our own modern philosophies and beliefs.[77]

Nietzsche rejoiced in heralding the news that the "age of belief" was over. In, *The Joyful Wisdom*, Nietzsche captures the essence of modern man's loss of religious belief via his famous 'Madman' character. In the work, the 'Madman' roams into a local town asking, "Have you ever heard of the madman who on a bright morning lighted a lantern and ran to the marketplace calling out unceasingly, "I seek God! I seek God!" – As there were many people standing about who did not believe in God, he caused a great deal of amusement. Why! Is he lost? Has he strayed away like a child? Or does he keep himself hidden?...the people cried out laughingly, all in a hubbub. The insane man jumped into their midst and transfixed them with his glance. "Where is God gone?" "I mean to tell you! We have killed him – you and I."

Yet, far from being distraught over the fact that God is now dead, Nietzsche beamed with gleeful anticipation at the opportunity for man to enjoy "full freedom" of expression. At last, argued Neitzsche, individuals would be liberated from rigid moralistic regulations and be free to express themselves without any hindrances or sanctions. In particular, Nietzsche saw this time in history as a period for the artist to undergo massive self-examination and emancipation. As he noted in his, *The Birth of Tragedy*, a "new" understanding of ancient Greek culture and art was needed to aid modern man in his liberation from similar simplistic artistic expression. Beckoning the artistic community to embrace the uninhibited and amoral "Dionysian" flavor of creativity, Neitzsche equated the "death of God" with unlimited license for artistry.

---

[77] Manuel Velasquez, *Philosophy* (Belmont, Wadsworth, 2002), 585.

Calling on the artists to flee the "Apollonian" restrictions of order and self-control, Nietzsche wanted the artist to know that the "death of God" meant that excess and extremism were now the order of the day. No longer dependent on or imprisoned by the "crutches" of accepted standards of morality, man could now celebrate and glory in his newfound autonomy. Finally, "free," the artist now answers to no rule, no person, and no standard – save himself.

Calling those that continued to "repress" their creative impulses by clinging to absolutes and self-control, "sheep," "shallow ponds," "the vulgar," or, most notably, "the herd," Nietzsche accused these types of failing to have confidence in their own abilities and humanness. Yet, there are those who wonder if it was wise to separate the arts from human dignity and ultimate purpose. After all, the classical understanding is that the arts are a powerful means of communicating something significant about reality, a means of representing truth.[78] As C. S. Lewis put it, "an author should never conceive of himself as bringing into existence beauty or wisdom which did not exist before, but simply and solely as trying to embody in terms of his own art some reflection of that eternal (absolute) Beauty and Wisdom."[79] In a 1999 address at the Wilberforce Conference, Chuck Colson corroborated Lewis' thoughts when he commented on the condition of Neitzsche's modern art phenomena. He stated, "Music, art, culture – they no longer have meaning if there are not absolutes of beauty and truth to which they can aspire and lift people. Art becomes whatever

---

[78] Chuck Colson, *How Now Shall We Live?* (Wheaton, Tyndale House, 1999), 441.
[79] Chuck Colson, *How Now Shall We Live?* (Wheaton, Tyndale House, 1999), 449.

someone says it is. The Virgin Mary, with dung hung on the picture. Is that art?"[80]

American philosopher Francis Schaeffer similarly has noted that, "Modern man has no moral imperative for what he *should do*, and consequently he is left only with what he *can do*.[81] In terms of how this affected artistic expression – adopting Nietzsche's freedom *from* any type of ideals – art went from glorifying absolute goodness, beauty, and truth to attacking and destroying any system of standards. This mentality is most clearly seen in an area most commonly associated with the French philosopher Jacques Derrida – the process of deconstruction. This method states that since there is no absolute truth, it logically follows that there can be no one "right" meaning in any work of art. In other words, any 'meaning' in a piece of art can now transcend the original intention of the author. Thus, the intended design and meaning of the artist actually becomes *subordinate* to that of the individual interpretation of the viewer. Similarly, Nietzsche's alleged freedom, interestingly enough, seemed to confine the modern artist to projects that were bent on protesting and denouncing any accepted universal standards. It is helpful to contrast this "new" attitude about artistic expression with what Aristotle once stated – "The aim of art is to represent not the outward appearance of things, but their *inward* significance." Modern-day author Chuck Colson, echoing the sentiments of Aristotle, plainly stated, "The whole-sale rejection of standards has led to the anti-art movement, exemplified by a 1993 exhibit titled, 'Abject Art' at the Whitney Art Museum in New York City. The exhibit

---

[80] Chuck Colson, *Chuck Colson Speaks* (Uhrichsville, Promise Press, 2000), 100.
[81] Francis Schaeffer, *The Complete Works of Francis Schaeffer, Volume Four* (Wheaton, Crossway Books, 1982), 76.

featured what its catalog described as 'abject materials such as dirt, hair, excrement, dead animals, menstrual blood, and rotting food.' The display included a three-foot mound of synthetic excrement, a dismembered sculpture of two women engaged in sexual acts, and a film depicting Jesus Christ as a naked woman...In other words, the artists had no higher aim than denouncing the beliefs and standards of ordinary people..."[82]

To further substantiate and promote the benefits of subjective expression, Nietzsche's brand of existentialism held that there was no single objective truth about the world. Therefore, according to Nietzsche, it logically follows that there cannot be a God or even a privileged perspective about truth. The best mankind could hope for, according to Nietzsche, would be each individual's reliance upon *some* truths that would enable day-to-day existence. In other words, even though there are no absolute truths – please refer to the earlier analysis of this contradictory statement – there are those truths that are "useful" as they help man live and gain power over the madness of total skepticism. Walking a definite tightrope, Nietzsche desperately tries to balance the notion of denying absolute truth with the pragmatic necessity of having basic "useful" truths. As Nietzsche put it, "Truth is that sort of error without which a particular type of living being could not live."[83] It should be pointed out that critics of Nietzsche view this "loophole" of selective "useful truths" as proof of the absurdity of relativism. To say it another way, without this convenient exemption of "useful truths," Nietzsche's world would be left with *no truths*, and thus in utter chaos and uncertainty.

---

[82] Chuck Coslon, *How Now Shall We Live?* (Wheaton, Tyndale House, 1999), 448.
[83] Manuel Velasquez, *Philosophy* (Belmont, Wadsworth, 2002), 586.

Of course, by gaining this self-imposed power (authority) of determining which "truths" are or are not necessary, one irrevocably places oneself at the center of all judgements. With truthfulness, now firmly resting in the hands of individual whim – or as Nietzsche prefers "interpretation" – it should come as no surprise that the floodgates protecting *meaning* and *truthfulness* were blown wide open for excess and abuse. In his work, *Truth – A History and a Guide for the Perplexed*, Felipe Fernandez-Armesto comments on the ramifications of this type of relativistic manipulation. He states, "Nietzsche insists that one interpretation should be preferred to another only if it is more self-fulfilling to the chooser. In this, as in all his repulsive doctrines, he was alone in his day but ominously representative of the future. In works mainly of the 1880's, he called for the reclassification of revenge, anger and lust as virtues, the rule of 'artist-tyrants', the refinement of the human race by gloriously bloody wars, the extermination of millions of inferior people, the eradication of Christianity with its contemptible bias to the weak, and an ethic of 'might is right'."[84] Consequently, Nietzsche's philosophically enlightened individual is one who successfully exploits and twists *truth* to his advantage. This individual does not have the hope of objective or absolute truth to aid him in his quest for meaning and measurement, but, rather, must rely only upon speculative and solitary manufacturing.

Yet, perhaps this deconstruction of objective truth was exactly what Nietzsche needed – or wanted – to do. By stripping truth away from any universal or absolute standard, Nietzsche conveniently paved the way to justify his ideals of power and exploitation under the banner of his "will to power." Taking a page from Schopenhauer's point of emphasis, Nietzsche, in his

---

[84] Felipe Fernandez-Armesto, *Truth: A History and a Guide for the Perplexed* (New York, Thomas Dunne, 1997), 176.

classic work, *Thus Spake Zarathustra*, turned the concept of the "Will" into something different and distinct. For Nietzsche, the faculty of reason had received far too much importance when it came to matters of metaphysics (questions about reality) and epistemology (questions about truth). Reason, he believed, is just a mask that one uses to disguise a primitive drive that controls one's cognitive life – and this drive he called the "will to power." It (the "will to power") manifests itself as the desire to overcome, to dominate one's environment, to make one's personal mark on the world, to create, or to express oneself.[85]

In this way, Nietzsche viewed every individual action or act as an outcome of the "will to power." People, then, for Nietzsche, are motivated out of a desire to increase their control over all that surrounds them. In *Beyond Good and Evil*, Nietzsche writes, "Life itself is essential assimilation, injury, violation of the foreign and the weaker, suppression, hardness, the forcing of one's own forms upon something else, ingestion and – at least in its mildest form – exploitation."[86] This "assimilation" and "suppression" came via Nietzsche's insistence that each individual move 'beyond' the narrow-minded definitions of *good* and *evil* by replacing these "out-dated" concepts with "new and improved" abstractions that only translate as *strong* and *weak*. Therefore, in accordance with Darwin's theory of "the survival of the fittest," human existence and morality would now be reduced to little more than a game between the "big fish" versus the "little fish." What humanity needed in order to survive in this entirely selfish and self-seeking environment, according to Nietzsche, was a new type of strong and

---

[85] William Lawhead, *The Philosophical Journey*, (Mountain View, Mayfield, 2000), 193.
[86] Friedrich Nietzsche, *Beyond Good and Evil* (New York, Vintage Books, 1966), 43.

dominant individual – a person who could overcome the timidity and weakness of the "herd morality." This person Nietzsche simply named the *overman*.

Nietzsche's *overman*, or as some translate it, "superman," is an individual who conquers his inner passions, drives, and fears to become a self-disciplined machine. By completely ignoring and denying the validity of normal human emotions, Nietzsche's *overman* egotistically marches through life proclaiming, "That which does not kill me only makes me stronger." This *overman* (over or beyond the average man) not only creates but also controls his own virtues and destiny. By combining the excessive strength of "the Roman Caesar" with the compassion of "Christ's soul," the *overman* becomes the master of his emotions, appetites, and surroundings. Nietzsche succinctly summarizes his job description for those applying to be an *overman*: "A human being who would be strong, highly educated, skillful in all bodily matters, self-controlled, reverent toward himself, and who might dare to afford the whole range and wealth of being natural, being strong enough for such freedom; the man of tolerance, not from weakness but from strength, because he knows how to use to his advantage, even that from which the average nature would perish; the man for whom there is no longer anything that is forbidden – unless it be weakness, whether called vice or virtue."[87]

As such, the *overman* is an individual who does not rely on any system of morality that placates to the common "herd" of everyday people. Rather, the *overman* rejects all procedures of ethical conformity, except his own, which he gladly uses to extend his sphere of influence over the unsuspecting masses. In the process, the *overman* rationalizes his self-centered

---

[87] William Lawhead, *The Voyage of Discovery, A Historical Introduction to Philosophy* (Belmont, Wadsworth, 2002), 428.

point of view largely because of his rejection of universal or absolute truth. Simply stated, since there are no absolute truths about the universe, there must not be any absolute truths about morality either – thus self-absorbed and self-indulgent attitudes are not only acceptable, they are necessary. Unlike the philosopher Kant, who emphasized morality was based on the categorical imperative of "ought implies must," Nietzsche and his self-created *overman* defined virtue within the parameters of individual advantage. Consequently, Nietzsche left man believing that since there are no moral facts or standards to speak of, the *overman* must create his own system of morality and truthfulness.

In his survey of the history of moralities, Nietzsche held that moralities were simply interpretations that were mere devices used to exert power over other individuals. Nietzsche believed that he had discovered two basic types of popular moralities. One kind was the "slave moralities" that weak people – especially the compassion laden Christians – had devised as instruments to acquire power over the strong. The other kind was the "master moralities" that had been devised by the strong to assert their power over the weak.[88] According to author Manuel Velasquez, the main difference between these groups was that the slave morality was invented by "weak" individuals to perpetuate feeble qualities, while the "master" morality actually developed inside stronger individuals. Thus, while the "master" morality praised qualities such as dominance, revenge, intelligence and strength, the slave morality valued the "lesser" traits of sympathy, kindness, patience, humility and helping those in need. This is precisely why Nietzsche referred to the "slave moralities" as those of

---

[88] Manuel Velasquez, *Philosophy* (Belmont, Wadsworth, 2002), 587.

the herd because they dared put the concerns of others before their own.

Yet, one must ask what type of world has Nietzsche left for mankind to live in. What is man to make of the universe and the question of ultimate purpose if morality and absolute truth are a fraud? Again, the strong influence of Arthur Schopenhauer is evident in the secular existential conclusions that Nietzsche makes about the significance of man. In *Essays and Aphorisms*, Schopenhauer laments, "All good things are vanity, the world in all its ends bankrupt, and life a business which does not cover its expenses. A quick test of the assertion that enjoyment outweighs pain in this world, or that they are at any rate balanced, would be to compare the feelings of an animal engaged in eating another with those of the animal being eaten." Not content to stop there, Schopenhauer continues to wax philosophical by embracing the doctrine of nihilism – namely that existence has no ultimate point or purpose. Continuing in *Essays and Aphorisms*, he states, "That human life must be some kind of mistake is sufficiently proved by the simple observation that man is a compound of needs which are hard to satisfy; that their satisfaction achieves nothing but a painless condition in which he is only given over to boredom; and that boredom is a direct proof that existence is in itself valueless, for boredom is nothing other than the sensation of the emptiness of existence."

Nietzsche concurred with this nihilistic approach to man's search for meaning with one glaring exception. While one side of his mouth was occupied uttering aphorisms about the emptiness of human existence, the other side was busy proclaiming that the *overman* could, nonetheless, still find life worth living. In other words, after taking the trouble to declare to the world that life is meaningless, Nietzsche's "superman" individual somehow manages to find existence worthwhile. George Orwell, in his famous *Nineteen Eighty-Four*, commented on this type of inconsistent rational: "Doublethink means the power of holding two contradictory beliefs simultaneously, and accepting both of them. The party intellectual knows that he is playing a trick with reality, but by the exercise of doublethink he also satisfies himself that reality is not violated."[89]   Albert Camus, himself an advocate of nihilism, was at least a bit more honest in his evaluation regarding the flimsy foundation of secular existentialism. Admitting the disparity in the absurdist, nihilistic position, Camus writes, "I proclaim that I believe in nothing and that everything is absurd, but I cannot doubt the validity of my own proclamation and I am compelled to believe, at least, in my own protest."[90]

To his credit, Nietzsche tried, perhaps harder than any person did, to live out his philosophy of meaninglessness to the end. He even went so far as to create a concept that he believed would provide some rational explanation to those stranded in this preposterous existence. Nietzsche referred to this "saving" theory as *eternal recurrence* – or the idea that when we die, we are fated to relive, over and over, every moment of our lives. In essence, Nietzsche was implying that throughout all eternity, man might be destined to repeat every act of his existence – painful or pleasurable – in an endless and absurd cycle of repetition. Echoing Nietzsche's nihilistic emphasis on perpetual meaninglessness, American philosopher Richard Taylor wrote words that could have just as easily come from the pen of Nietzsche himself. In his work, *The Meaning of Life*, Taylor states, "We toil after goals, most of them – indeed every single one of them

---

[89] Colin Chapman, *The Case for Christianity* (Grand Rapids, Eerdman's, 1981), 208.
[90] Colin Chapman, *The Case for Christianity* (Grand Rapids, Eerdman's, 1981), 212.

– of transitory significance and, having gained one of them, we immediately set forth for the next, as if that one had never been, with this next one being essentially more of the same. Look at a busy street any day, and observe the throng going hither and thither. To what? Some office or shop, where the same things will be done today as were done yesterday, and are done now so they may be repeated tomorrow...our achievements, even though they are often beautiful, are mostly bubbles."[91]

For Nietzsche, the doctrine of eternal recurrence is far more than just a trite philosophical theory. In fact, the very idea of eternal recurrence is nothing less than an essential psychological test that allows each individual to gage his emotional response to the possibility of recurrent redundancy. By candidly accepting the prospect of recurrence, one is inevitably driven to either heights of despair or joy. For Nietzsche, this head-on confrontation with *reality* is a blessing in disguise. Only when one truly weighs the prospect of the 'universe' and the 'self' as having no ultimate purpose, can one begin to appreciate the necessity of the *overman*. Thus, the doctrine of eternal recurrence brilliantly shows the lack of ultimate meaning in man's day-to-day petty existence, while also serving as a catalyst for the *overman* individual to live his life in the face of such repetitive nothingness. In other words, the authentic secular existentialist knows that *Life* offers no hope or purpose, yet continues to live on. Therefore, according to Nietzsche, the bona fide existential individual, or the *overman*, fully embraces the possibility of eternal recurrence and triumphantly "overcomes" the human psychological need to find any ultimate *meaning*.

---

[91] Manuel Velasquez, *Philosophy* (Belmont, Wadsworth, 2002), 710.

Despite his zealous declarations, one cannot help but wonder about the legitimacy or practicality of Nietzsche's advice in trying to "overcome" basic human psychological needs. In fact, many view this "overcoming" as simple denial. Perhaps individuals *have* basic psychological needs – like a desire to know why we exist – because these needs serve a specific purpose, namely to direct man toward something beyond his own perceptions. Yet, as Nietzsche continued to deny these fundamental human longings, he systematically plunged modern man down a road of apathetic uncertainty. Commenting on the influence of Nietzsche's philosophy, Colin Wilson states, "Most of these poets of the late nineteenth century were only half in love with easeful death; the other half clung firmly to life and complained about its futility...but follow their pessimism further, press it to the limits of complete sincerity, and the result is a completely life-denying nihilism that is actually a danger to life. When Van Gogh's 'Misery will never end' is combined with Evan Strowde's 'Nothing is worth doing', the result is a kind of spiritual syphilis that can hardly stop short of death or insanity."[92]

It is interesting to note, whether the result of constant physical illness, or a tormented soul, Friedrich Nietzsche would eventually go mad and live his last eleven years on earth in stages of insanity. One cannot help but be reminded of the main character in Joseph Conrad's existential work, *Heart of Darkness*, when considering Nietzsche's final years. Again, Colin Wilson remarks, "Joseph Conrad's story *Heart of Darkness* deals with a man who has brought himself to this point; he dies murmuring: 'The horror, the horror.' Conrad's narrator comments: '...I wasn't arguing with a lunatic either...His intelligence was perfectly clear;

---

[92] Colin Chapman, *The Case for Christianity* (Grand Rapids, Eerdman's, 1981), 190.

concentrated...upon himself with a horrible intensity, yet clear...But his soul was mad. Being alone in the Wilderness, it had looked within itself, and ...it had gone mad: he had summed up; he had judged: the Horror.'"[93] As H. J. Blackham suggests, "In his own case, he (Nietzsche) provided himself with no means of getting out of nihilism into which he plunged himself, precisely because it was a deliberate plunge over the edge. He tried to say at the same time: nihilism must be surmounted; nihilism cannot be surmounted; nihilism is good; nihilism is best. He imprisoned himself within the chalked circle of his own metaphysical assumptions."[94] According to philosopher Alasdair MacIntyre, "The end result of Nietzsche's deconstruction of morality was not a race of *over-men* saying yes to life in a world beyond good and evil, but a world of people clinging to a thin notion of right and wrong that rests on a purely emotional basis, not a rational or empirical one."[95]

Before Nietzsche died on August 25, 1900, he would spend his final years of declining health dealing with bouts of extreme personal loneliness. Having isolated himself over the years, Nietzsche even found his several marriage proposals being soundly rejected by the women he solicited. From 1889, the year the desolate philosopher went mad, to his dying day, the proud advocate of the individual "superman" existed under the mercy of his indulgent sister. Author Felipe Fernandez-Armesto in *Truth – A History and a Guide for the Perplexed*, reflects on Nietzsche's life and contribution to philosophy. He writes, "His was a typical, if extreme, case of the enmity of promise: he

---

[93] Colin Chapman, *The Case for Christianity* (Grand Rapids, Eerdman's, 1981), 190.
[94] Colin Chapman, *The Case for Christianity* (Grand Rapids, Eerdman's, 1981), 189.
[95] Chuck Colson, *Chuck Colson Speaks* (Uhrichsville, Promise Press, 2000), 66.

was praised too much in his youth for his superior powers of mind and never achieved prowess or position to match. His life was confined to a dull provincial chair and a succession of sanatoria. A sexually inexperienced invalid, he advocated the exploitation of women 'for the recreation of the warrior.' Like Hitler, Nietzsche hated people but loved animals. He fell defending an abused horse. His prescription for the world was a morbid fantasy, warped and mangled out of his own lonely, sickly self-hatred...(it was) a twisted vision from the edge of insanity."[96]

In turning to the other notable secular existential thinker, Jean-Paul Sartre, we are confronted with the awesome realization that man is responsible for all that he does – he is "absolutely free." As such, man must realize that he does not "have" or possess freedom, but rather, he "is" freedom. For Sartre, who actually named the movement of existentialism, this necessarily means that there cannot be a sovereign God or established system of universal truth because the mere existence of an eternal Being would interfere with the propriety of freedom. Consequently, an enormous burden of individual responsibility is thrust upon every person resulting in Sartre's notion that man is "condemned to be free." We are free because we can rely neither on God nor on society to justify our actions or to tell us what we essentially are. We are condemned because without a fixed purpose or a guideline we must suffer the agony of our own decision making and the anguish of its consequences.[97] As a result, according to Sartre, there are no ultimate values to be discovered in any factual or objective realm, leaving each individual to create his own essence and

---

[96] Felipe Fernandez-Armesto, *Truth – A History and a Guide for the Perplexed* (New York, Thomas Dunne Books, 1997), 177.
[97] Manuel Velasquez, *Philosphy* (Belmont, Wadsworth, 2002), 96.

meaning by continually choosing responsible modes of behavior.

Much of Sartre's thoughts have already been highlighted in this work; however, it is necessary to elaborate a bit more on both the man and his work. Ever popular for his philosophical essays, plays, novels and short stories, Sartre also attracted attention because of his affection for the Communist Party. Living most of his adult life out of different hotel rooms while refusing to succumb to the "bourgeois snare of matrimony," Sartre preferred to spend his time thinking and writing in the Left Bank sidewalk cafes of Paris. Having been raised as an isolated and detached youth in his grandparents' home, Sartre would die in 1980 in much the same way – cut off from the mainstream. With a mass collection of books, few friends, and his live-in girlfriend by his side, Sartre died a self-fulfilling prophecy. Earlier in his life, the renowned secular existentialist Jean-Paul Sartre had calmly stated, "I began my life, as I shall no doubt end it: amidst books."

Jean-Paul Sartre's philosophy of existentialism begins with the skepticism of the agnostic whose attitudes are described by a character in his novel *Nausea*: "I am beginning to believe that nothing can ever be proved. These are reasonable hypotheses which take the facts into account: but I am only too well aware that they come from me, that they are simply a way of unifying my own knowledge."[98] With these words, Sartre begins to formulate his ideas regarding the human condition in a universe – as he sees it – apart from meaning and direction. Sartre was born in Paris in 1905 and attained fame as a writer when his work, *Nausea*, became a best seller. Having lost his father when he was a young boy, Sartre grew up a lonely child who turned to writing as his favorite outlet

---

[98] Colin Chapman, *The Case for Christianity* (Grand Rapids, Eerdman's, 1981), 193.

for comfort. This passion for composition led Sartre in the natural direction during his later years to develop a relationship with the feminist author Simone de Beauvoir. Though they never married, the two spent what could best be described as a "mutually convenient" fifty-one year relationship together. Throughout these years, Sartre would go on to write voluminously about his views on man and his predicament in a seemingly pointless and absurd universe. To this end, Jean-Paul Sartre was and is regarded by many as the chief exponent of atheistic existentialism based on his rejection of God and the fundamental denial of any essential human nature.

By putting aside absolute truth or any type of universal standard, Sartre embraced philosophical relativism by placing the individual at the center of all situations. Declaring that there is no *meaning* to the world apart from the *meaning* that each person creates, Sartre enjoined his students to formulate their own versions of truth. In one instance, Sartre boldly announced, "You are free, therefore choose – that is to say, invent." Sartre continues by adding, "This is the idea I shall try to convey when I say that man is condemned to be free. Condemned, because he did not create himself, yet, in other respects is free; because, once thrown into the world, he is responsible for everything he does. Man is nothing else than his plan; he exists only to the extent that he fulfills himself."[99]

Sartre envisioned the world as a place where each individual person "invents" his or her own version of what is right, wrong, true or false. Sartre insisted that each person is the *center* of the universe and, as such, must "play God" by disbursing meaning and significance to whatever values, he or she deems

---

[99] Joan A. Price, *Philosophy Through the Ages* (Belmont, Wadsworth, 2000), 473-474.

appropriate. The logical result of this type of existence, for Sartre, is not a hedonistic and self-centered people but, rather, a society of "fulfilled" individuals. Yet, even when man does seem to find some degree of self-fulfillment, Sartre warns that these feelings of satisfaction are short-lived. Because man is alone and resides in a universe that is without significance, Sartre contends that feelings of fear and anguish are not only normal, but also simply unavoidable. Sartre defines the state of 'anguish' as the emotions that are encountered when considering actions that one might do in the future. In contrast, the state of 'fear' deals with the emotions one has when considering what actions might happen to one personally. As an individual becomes more aware of his personal freedom and the enormous responsibility that accompanies it, Sartre stated that feelings of anguish would naturally follow.

In *The Humanist Glossary*, the section dealing with (secular) existentialism states, "The starting point of existentialist philosophy is the plight of the individual thrust, as it were, into a world without authority, system of values, of law or human nature. Their basic tenet is that there is an inescapable tension between thought and existence...Man, being both thinker and in existence, has to live this tension, which he can never resolve once for all."[100] Jean-Paul Sartre adds that, "The first effect of (secular) existentialism is that it puts every man in possession of himself as he is, and places the entire responsibility for his existence squarely upon his own shoulders. And, when we say that man is responsible for himself, we do not mean

---

[100] Colin Chapman, *The Case for Christianity* (Grand Rapids, Eerdman's, 1981), 209.

that he is responsible only for his own individuality, but that he is responsible for all men."[101]

Perhaps this is why Sartre concluded that man is "a useless passion" and that all of life is an empty bubble on the sea of nothingness. In his novel *Nausea*, the protagonist Roquentin sees life in its nakedness...and suddenly discovers that being, as it reveals itself in the crisis of consciousness, is pure superfluity, pure excess, and obscene disorder. There ✳ is no reason to exist yet we do exist, and we exist in an absurd and meaningless world.[102]

It is not surprising that Jean-Paul Sartre placed such an enormous emphasis on individual choices and responsibility when one considers his personal involvement in World War II. After being captured, Sartre spent nearly a year of confinement in a Nazi prison camp where he actually wrote and produced plays for fellow prisoners. Surrounded by continual suffering, death, and fear, Sartre no doubt formulated his philosophical thoughts with a bent towards emphasizing individual consciousness and accountability. Sartre stresses, "Man will do nothing unless he has first understood that he must count on no one but himself; that he is alone, abandoned on earth in the midst of his infinite responsibilities; without help, with no other aim than the one he sets himself, with no other destiny than the one he forges for himself on this earth."[103] For Sartre, then, the central point of philosophy is that human beings are always free to choose how they respond to any given situation. He boldly announces in *Being and Nothingness*, "Thus there are no accidents in life; a community event

---

[101] Colin Chapman, *The Case for Christianity* (Grand Rapids, Eerdman's, 1981), 210.
[102] Joan A. Price, *Philosophy Through the Ages* (Belmont, Wadsworth, 2000), 469.
[103] Manuel Velasquez, *Philosophy* (Belmont, Wadsworth, 2002), 98.

suddenly bursts forth and involves me in it...if I am mobilized in a war, this war is *my* war; it is in my image and I deserve it. I deserve it first because I could always get out of it by suicide or by desertion...for lack of getting out of it, I have *chosen* it." Professor Robert Solomon of the University of Texas clearly and concisely summarizes Sartre's theme of individual choice. He writes, "Against all such excuses, Sartre wants to argue that we are absolutely free. We are responsible for what we do, what we are, and the way our world is."

In his essay, *Existentialism is a Humanism*, Sartre presents his readers with the idea of "existence precedes essence." For Sartre, this means that first we exist as beings and then we produce our own nature. Therefore, one's uniqueness and self-worth are not predetermined but, rather, depend on how one chooses to act – in other words, we are born with no nature or meaning and we give ourselves purpose only by our actions. By exclaiming that there is no specific essence that defines what it is to be human, Sartre willingly opposed the medieval philosophers who staunchly held that "essence precedes existence." Thinkers such as Aquinas and Augustine taught that an individual instantaneously had 'essence' – that which makes an entity what it is – because of the possession of a rational soul. In other words, each human being *has* meaning and importance from conception and lives only to give existence to an already given essence. Sartre, however, insists otherwise when he states, "What do we mean by saying that existence precedes essence? We mean that man first of all exists, encounters himself, surges up in the world – and defines himself afterwards...Man is nothing else but that which he makes himself."[104] If you are thinking

---

[104] Colin Chapman, *The Case for Christianity* (Grand Rapids, Eerdman's, 1981), 209.

that you have heard this message before – the directive for man to define his own values and worth – recall Protagoras and his "Man is the measure of all things" mantra.

Before Jean-Paul Sartre died in 1980, he had plenty of time to lament the fact that his was a life of "books and theory" instead of action. Content to watch life from the sidewalk coffee shops, free from the "entanglements" of a wife or children, Sartre saw fit to pronounce life as meaningless. Rather than embracing human relationships, Sartre conveniently chose to isolate himself and simply "re-define" friendship and associations as mere struggles for self-definition. Sartre even went so far, through one of his characters in his play *No Exit*, to denounce the benefits of friendship by having the character proclaim, "Hell is – other people." Therefore, instead of giving himself totally to one person in a loving relationship, Sartre chose to "authenticate" himself with a continual succession of lovers – all while still living with girlfriend Simone. Thus, Sartre selfishly reduced the emotion of love to a seductive strategy rather than an act of selfless devotion. In a glaring contradiction, Sartre contends in his philosophical theories that a romantic relationship is nothing more than a vehicle by which one can manipulate and control another. Sex, for example, has little to do with pleasure and more to do with domination and exploitation. If this is so, why did Sartre find it necessary – or convenient – to stay with Simon for over fifty years? One may justifiably ask, "What are we to make of a philosopher who theorizes in one direction yet lives in quite another?"

Chapter Six

- They deem him their worst enemy who tells them the truth.

- Plato

On November 22, 1963, the world lost three of the most influential individuals that have ever walked among us: John F. Kennedy (President of the United States), Aldous Huxley (author of *Brave New World*), and Oxford don, Clive Staples (C. S.) Lewis (distinguished author and absolutist apologist). Despite all three men having very different professions, they all, nonetheless, made an indelible mark on Western civilization. Although more than a generation has passed, people are still reading Huxley's masterpiece and quoting Kennedy's "Ask not what your country can do for you" speech. As for Lewis' legacy, all thirty-eight of his books have never been out of print and continue to be purchased worldwide at a rate of 1.5 million copies a year.

C. S. Lewis' writings show both the depth and magnitude of the man who would author books and essays in the fields of science fiction, philosophy, theology, poetry, and children's literature. Close to Lewis' heart was his earnest striving to take his readers away from "Modern" and "Post-Modern" assumptions about thought and bring them back to the basics of ancient and medieval philosophical assurance. During this quest to defend absolute truth – "permanent things" – C. S. Lewis continually served as a spokesman for the *philosophia perennis* – the perennial philosophy shaped by Greek philosophers such as Plato and Aristotle, and by medieval theologians such as Augustine and Thomas Aquinas...thinkers who blended

69

moral realism, natural law, divine law, and the ethics of virtue into the central ethical tradition of Western civilization.[105]

For Lewis, the central point of all philosophical inquiry focuses upon the question of universal law. Is there an absolute – or universal – law of right and wrong, truth or falsehood, which has existed in all cultures? It is on this point of contention that Lewis is uniquely qualified to offer insight because he served as a spokesman for both points of view. Having spent the first thirty-two years of his life as a non-religious existential thinker and teacher, Lewis was all too familiar with relativistic perceptions. Yet, throughout those years, Lewis inwardly battled with a concept that would gnaw at his heart and intellect, eventually causing him to abandon all previously held beliefs. The idea that so dramatically influenced Lewis was the notion of the ancient *Tao* – or an absolute reality or universal standard of rightness and order. All major cultures since the beginning of history have understood this concept of a universal order – all, that is, except postmodern Western culture. Despite the differences among them, all major civilizations have believed in a divine order that lays down the law for both natural and human realms. In the Far East it was called *Tao*; in ancient Egypt it was called *Ma'at*; in Greek philosophy it was called *Logos*.[106] Therefore, inasmuch as Lewis wanted to remain a supporter of relativistic thinking, one elementary question continued to plague his mind: "Where does humanity's moral and seemingly universal code of behavior come from?"

Disagreeing with Nietzsche, Lewis, according to author Armand Nicholi, argued that ethics are not a

---

[105] Gerard Reed, *C. S. Lewis Explores Vice and Virtue* (Kansas City, Beacon Hill Press, 2001), 13.
[106] Chuck Colson, *How Now Shall We Live?* (Wheaton, Tyndale House 1999), 297.

product of human engineering but, rather, are universal, constant, and cross-cultural. In his writings, Lewis elaborated upon his belief that absolute moral truth transcended time, culture, and applied to all. In verifying the existence of objective truth, Lewis compared the moral teachings of the ancient Egyptians, Babylonians, Hindus, Chinese, Greeks, and Romans and found "how very like they are to each other and to our own...Think of a country where people were admired for running away in battle, or where a man felt proud of double-crossing all the people who had been kind to him...Men have differed in regards to what people you ought to be unselfish to – whether it was only your family, or your fellow countrymen, or everyone. But they have always agreed that you ought not put yourself first. Selfishness has never been admired."[107]

In his apologetic masterpiece, *Mere Christianity*, Lewis further explores the issue of universal truth via his example of how people react when they are told a lie or have something stolen from them. Noting that people forever argue, Lewis observed that in the process they invoke a *standard* they all accept. Without some "natural law" to which all of us appeal, we could have no arguments – why *object* to someone's behavior unless it is *wrong*?[108] According to Lewis, a person who is defrauded or cheated, regardless of the time in history or geographical location, will respond with sentiments of, "Hey, that's not fair!" "You've wronged me!" Lewis maintains that we must ask, "From where did these standards – or code – of rightness and fairness originate? Lewis explains, "You call a boy's answer to a sum *wrong*

---

[107] Armand M. Nicholi, *The Question of God* (New York, The Free Press, 2002), 61.
[108] Gerard Reed, *C. S. Lewis Explores Vice and Virtue* (Kansas City, Beacon Hill Press, 2001), 18.

because you know the *right* answer. You call a man cruel or idle because you have in mind a standard of kindness or diligence. If you begin to doubt the standard, you automatically doubt the cogency of your accusation."[109]   Thus, strongly disagreeing with relativistic philosophers, Lewis contends that man does not simply "make up" these standards or codes to suit his societal needs or wishes. Rather, man *discovers* this code – the *Tao* or universal truth – much in the same manner that he uncovers the laws of mathematics. In other words, universal truth is something that mankind "finds" and not something that he creates. To say it another way, Lewis believes that just because one learns the principles of multiplication, this does not mean that one created or "made up" the entire system of mathematical principles – discovery is not invention.

If Lewis is correct about absolute or universal truth being *discovered* and not invented, then one must recognize that "proof" of transcendent truth is beyond observable notation. To this end, Lewis argued against the scientific method – a formula that states the *only* source of knowledge is that which can be observed – as being the sole response for epistemological (what is the source of knowledge) concerns. As Harvard psychiatrist Dr. Armand Nicholi has written, Lewis believed that the scientific method could not possibly answer all philosophical questions because it – science – is not the *source* of all knowledge. For instance, Lewis points out that while science can report on what it *observes*, it cannot, however, tell us anything about *why* something comes to be. Lewis continues: "We want to know whether the universe simply happens to be what it is for no reason or whether there is a power (source) behind it that makes it what it is...(this power

[109] Gerard Reed, *C. S. Lewis Explores Vice and Virtue* (Kansas City, Beacon Hill Press, 2001), 19.

shows itself) inside ourselves as an influence or a command trying to get us to behave in a certain way. And that is just what we do find inside ourselves...something which is directing the universe and which appears in me as a law (code) urging me to do right and making me feel responsible and uncomfortable when I do wrong."[110]

C. S. Lewis fully understood that the relativist and secular existentialist would protest that ideas of "right and wrong" are nothing more than human creations handed down to us by our parents. Author Armand Nicholi points out that while Lewis agrees that some morality is indeed learned, this does not mean, or imply, that *Truth* is a man-made entity. Lewis argues that parents did not make up *Truth* or truthfulness any more than they invented the multiplication tables, which they also taught us. Lewis insists that since the beginning of recorded history people have been aware of a law (code) that they felt they *ought* to obey. Where did this feeling of *ought* come from? Lewis concludes, "All the human beings that history has heard of acknowledged some kind of morality; that is, they feel towards certain proposed actions the experiences expressed by the words 'I ought' or 'I ought not.' And they usually fail to live up to this law (code or standard). First...human beings, all over the earth, have this curious idea that they ought to behave in a certain way, and cannot really get rid of it. Secondly...they *do not* in fact behave in that way...These two facts are the foundation of all clear thinking about ourselves and the universe we live in."[111] The author Tolstoy summed it up in a similar fashion when he asked, "Why do I know what is right and do what is wrong?"

---

[110] Armand M. Nicholi, *The Question of God* (New York, The Free Press, 2002), 59.
[111] Armand M. Nicholi, *The Question of God* (New York, The Free Press, 2002), 61.

As C. S. Lewis continued to develop his religious existential views, he made it clear that he feared for the future of Western civilization. The more he looked at the condition of "modern" man, the more evident it became that "enlightened" humanity had become comfortable with the disposing of absolute truth. Lewis realized that post-modern man had seen fit to cast aside the ancient wisdom of Plato and Aristotle, thereby replacing reason with mere feelings and an over-emphasis on personal pleasure. According to Professor Gerard Reed, C. S. Lewis condemned the creeping excesses of our sensate culture by warning that if each of us composes his or her own bill of rights, claiming "rights" to collect undeserved dividends and indulge in unlimited pleasures...we will slide into a world in which everyone will insist on his or her own way and implode the common culture...[112] Maintaining that personal happiness is *independent* of pleasures, Lewis held that individuals had a right to seek happiness so long as they understood that this did not mean that they had an inherit *right* to happiness itself. Commenting on those who insisted that they held some innate right to blissfulness, Lewis replied, "This sounds to me as odd as a right to good luck." He continued, "We depend for a very great deal of our happiness or misery on circumstances outside of our control. A right to happiness doesn't, for me, make much more sense than a right to be six feet tall, or to have a millionaire for your father or to get good weather whenever you want to have a picnic."[113]

As for the exaggerated importance placed on individual gratification, Harvard psychiatrist Dr. Armand Nicholi insists that Lewis noted how the concepts of

---

[112] Gerard Reed, *C. S. Lewis Explores Vice and Virtue* (Kansas City, Beacon Hill Press, 2001), 14.
[113] Armand M. Nicholi, *The Question of God* (New York, The Free Press, 2002), 105.

"repression" and "suppression" were usually part of the discussion. For this reason, Lewis believed that these terms needed serious contemplation and consideration. While concluding that repression is an unconscious process that can lead to unhealthy conditions, suppression of one's desires, on the other hand, was simply a conscious control of one's inclinations. Lewis, arguing for the implementation of self-imposed balanced suppression, claimed that far too many individuals believed that an impulse, or desire, denoted an immediate *right* for gratification. Yet, Lewis spoke out against this type of inauthentic living. For Lewis, a life lived without continual examination and self-control had only one realistic outcome. Lewis remarked, "Surrender to all our desires obviously leads to...disease, jealousy, lies, concealment and everything that is the reverse of health...For any happiness, even in this world, quite a lot of restraint is going to be necessary..."[114]

Like Aristotle, C. S. Lewis saw the satisfaction of personal desires and pleasure in the context of fulfilling a proper function – or according to natural law. As Aristotle had taught centuries before, Lewis, too, supported and furthered the notion that all "things" had a specific function and purpose – the idea of *entelechy* or natural objects having a built-in natural end. As author Joan Price points out, "Aristotle called this process 'entelechy', which is the Greek word for "to become its essence...Entelechy means that nothing happens by chance. Nature not only has a built-in pattern, but also different levels of being"[115] For example, an acorn is created and exists for a precise purpose – to mature into an oak tree. For Lewis,

---

[114] Armand M. Nicholi, *The Question of God* (New York, The Free Press, 2002), 136.
[115] Joan Price, *Philosophy Through the Ages* (Belmont, Wadsworth, 2000), 75.

human desires, appetites and pleasures are no different and must be understood in much the same way. In other words, individual desires for specific pleasures should be satisfied in the context of their intended end or purpose.

However, when a craving or a desire is appeased outside the boundaries of that desires designed function, discontent and ultimate disillusionment eventually set in. Lewis provided the following illustration to show just how ludicrous one's actions can become when pleasures are pursued uncontrolled and are separated from their intended function. Lewis writes, "You can get a large audience together for a strip-tease act – that is to watch a girl undress on the stage. Now suppose you came to a country where you could fill a theater by simply bringing a covered plate onto a stage and then *slowly* lifting the cover so as to let every one see, just before the lights went out, that it contained a mutton chop or a bit of bacon. Would you not think that in that country something had gone wrong with food?"[116]

Like the ancient Greco-Roman philosophers, Lewis drew a distinct and clear connection between happiness and virtuous living. He fully embraced the ancient ideal that dedication to virtuous living was not only the way to good health but also the secret to *true* happiness. It should be pointed out that Lewis, again adhering to the wisdom of the ancient philosophers, understood *happiness* as the reward one inherits from living a virtuous life. The Greek word, *eudaimonia*, best captures this sentiment by stressing that happiness is not something associated with mere sensual pleasures or materialism – in other words, happiness is not an event or toy. Rather, genuine happiness is a "state of life" revolving around

---

[116] Armand M. Nicholi, *The Question of God* (New York, The Free Press, 2002), 138.

contemplation and the perfecting of the inner man. To say it another way, happiness results from achieving excellence in the fulfillment of one's function or purpose.

Following the lead of Aristotle's notion that all things "aim" at a *good*, or teleology, Lewis also taught that everything and every person has a definite design – or purpose. Thus, as the ancients ever taught, life was not simply about living, but about *living well*. Therefore, it should come as no surprise, according to Lewis, that when humanity properly understands the relationship between virtue and personal happiness, they will also quite naturally be concerned with questions about *moral philosophy*. For example, man should ponder his happiness by asking questions such as, "How can I be good?" "What is the good in life?" "What is the *summum bonum* or greatest good at which I should be aiming at?" Only in this context can the existential individual fully comprehend the totality of *happiness* and come to appreciate the words of Immanuel Kant when he said, "Morality is not properly the doctrine of how we make ourselves happy, but how we make ourselves worthy of happiness." Like the ancient philosophers, C. S. Lewis answered that individual happiness was – and is – intrinsically related to an individual fulfilling his or her function as a person. For Lewis, this naturally meant that people must be about the task of discovering their function, purpose, talents, and unique gifts. This type of existential existence, far from being effortless or automatic, requires a life-long commitment and pursuit to authenticity. Still, Lewis believed that anything short of this kind of lifestyle was, at best, a shallow fraud.

In other various public addresses and lectures, Lewis argued that modernism – with its emphasis on having each individual define happiness, truth, right or wrong – would not only destroy thousands of years of classical philosophy, but mankind's very existence as well. By dismissing universal truth – or an absolute standard – Lewis argued that the floodgates would open to an onslaught of relativistic or subjective thinking. In an article written in 1943 entitled, *The Poison of Subjectivism*, C. S. Lewis wrote, "The very idea of freedom presupposes some objective moral law, which overarches rulers and ruled alike. Subjectivism (read relativism) of values is eternally incompatible with democracy. We and our rulers are of one kind only so long as we are subject to one law, but if there is no law of nature, the ethos of any society is the creation of its rulers, educators, and conditioners. Unless we return to the crude and nursery-like belief in objective values, we perish."[117]

For C. S. Lewis, nothing was more important than championing philosophical realism in the defense of objective or absolute *Truth*. Accordingly, Lewis staunchly maintained, "If Truth is objective, if we live in a world we did not create and cannot change merely by thinking, if the world is not really a dream of our own, then the most destructive belief we could possibly believe would be the denial of this primary fact. It would be like closing your eyes while driving, or blissfully ignoring the doctor's warning."[118] Indeed, the battle of absolute or objective *Truth* over relativistic and subjective interpretation was a matter of life and death for Lewis. He viewed subjective philosophy as "a disease that will certainly end our species and...damn our souls if it is not crushed (along with) the fatal superstition that men can create values, (or) that a community can choose its 'ideology' as men choose their clothes."[119]

---

[117] Chuck Colson, *Chuck Colson Speaks* (Uhrichsville, Promise Press, 2000), 207.
[118] Gerard Reed, *C. S. Lewis Explores Vice and Virtue* (Kansas City, Beacon Hill Press, 2001), 130.
[119] Gerard Reed, *C. S. Lewis Explores Vice and Virtue* (Kansas City, Beacon Hill Press, 2001), 15.

In his philosophical classic, *The Abolition of Man*, C. S. Lewis soundly speaks out against the supposition that all values are subjective and that truth must be defined by emotions. Lewis firmly held that in order for an individual to live a singularly authentic existence, that person must recognize that humanity's code of ethics – the *Tao, Ma'at, Logos* – is not a product of man-made manufacturing. When man discards the objectivity of *Truth* and loses his ethical foundation, Lewis submits that the universe is left with nothing less than "the abolition of man." In fact, Lewis declared that we – 'Post-modern Western civilization' – have already started on the insidious deconstruction of man by creating generation after generation of "men without chests." By this, Lewis simply meant that relativistic thinking and philosophy has produced individuals devoid of virtue because they lack the capacity to reconcile the inclinations of the head (reason) and the stomach (appetites). The "chest," to which Lewis was referring, is critically important and vital to the overall welfare of each individual because it serves as the *mediator* between the tendencies of the head and the passions of the gut. In other words, man's "chest" is nothing less than his heart, soul, and conscience waging battle against the excesses of reason and instinct.

According to Lewis, when we reduce absolute *Truth* or universal standards to continual subjective interpretation, we destroy an individual's "chest" and leave him powerless in his hopes of living a life of virtue. The moment the "chest" is abolished or destroyed, nothing remains to guard against the excesses of man's imaginations or cravings. Thus, with no "chest" or standard to guide his desires, appetites, ideas, or opinions, the individual is completely vulnerable to his own, as well as outside, manipulations. Noted sociologist Pitrim Sorokin sums up the plight of this condition by remarking, "If a person has no strong convictions as to what is right and what is wrong, if he does not believe in any God or absolute moral values, what can guide and control his conduct toward other men? Nothing but his desires and lusts. Under these conditions he loses all rational and moral control, even plain common sense."[120]

In the end, C. S. Lewis concluded that if transcendent universal standards exist, there must be an eternal Provider responsible for their actuality. The evidence for such a Provider or Creator, according to Lewis, can be found within the existence of basic human longings and desires. In his autobiographical work, *Surprised by Joy*, Lewis discusses the issue of individual cravings by citing the German expression *Sehnsucht* to describe periods of longing that human beings encounter throughout their lives. Lewis frequently used the word *joy* to describe these brief yearnings and defined these episodes of longing as "intense desires for that which is just outside or beyond one's grasp." *Joy*, then, is simply an overwhelming desire for something beyond a person's possession – something higher than himself. Lewis asserts that this understanding of *Sehnsucht* highlights the notion that mere earthly pleasures were never meant to satisfy man's deepest and innermost longings. As for the existence of human desires, Lewis stated that individual beings usually possess desires for things that *actually* exist. Lewis explains, "Creatures are not born with desires unless satisfaction for those desires exists. A baby feels hunger: well, there is such a thing as food. A duckling wants to swim: well, there is such a thing as water. Men feel sexual desire: well, there is such a thing as sex." Lewis then piercingly brings the discussion of human desires and deep-seated longings full-circle by addressing mankind's most personal and

---

[120] Gerard Reed, *C. S. Lewis Explores Vice and Virtue* (Kansas City, Beacon Hill Press, 2001), 17.

consequential uncertainty – the desire to avoid death and live forever. He concludes the matter by pointedly suggesting, "If I find myself having a desire which no experience in *this* world can satisfy (the desire to live forever), the most probable explanation is that I was made for *another* world."[121]

---

[121] Armand M. Nicholi, *The Question of God* (New York, The Free Press, 2002), 47.

Chapter Seven

*- The ancient Greek philosophers, such as
Epicurus, Zeno, and Socrates, remained more faithful
to the Idea of the philosopher than their modern
counterparts have done. "When will you finally begin to
live virtuously?" said Plato to an old man who told him
he was attending classes on virtue. The point is not
always to speculate, but also ultimately to think about
applying our knowledge. Today, however, he who lives
in conformity with what he teaches is taken for a
dreamer.*
— *Immanuel Kant*

After six chapters we find ourselves back at the
place where we first began – asking, "What is THE BIG
PICTURE?" "What is the point of my existence?"
"Does my life have any meaning or purpose?" "How
can I find fulfillment in a world so overflowing with
confusion and disappointment?" As stated earlier, the
search for the answers to these questions is
inseparable from an understanding of what it means to
be fully human. The ancient masters, Plato and
Aristotle, figured out a long time ago that mankind
could not divide how they *lived* from how they *thought* if
they were genuinely seeking authenticity from their
lives. Repeatedly these Greek educators pushed their
students to fully embrace and participate in the glorious
quest "for the good life." In other words, *philosophy* –
or the love of truth – was not merely a college course –
it was a way of life.

Sadly, our post-modern world has seen fit to
keep the "absolutist" thinkers such as Plato, Aristotle,
Aquinas, Pascal, Dostoevsky, Tolkien, C. S. Lewis, and
countless others, on the shelves of our libraries.

Convincing us for generations that objective or absolute *Truth* is an obsolete concept from an archaic age, they instead have heralded relativism and skepticism as man's only hope for personal fulfillment. Yet, in his haste to make man the center of the universe, the post-modern intellectual overlooked one very important possibility. If man can make up his own rules and version of truth, then he can also *change* his truth and *break* his rules to accommodate any and all ambitions.

The modern embracing of relativism (the idea that the only truth that exists is *the truth* that each individual creates) has not been without consequence. By taking universal truth hostage, the relativist placed mankind in a most absurd predicament – man was now declared to be *both* the problem *and* the solution to all the world's evils. With no objective standard or absolutes to guide him on his journey, modern man turned to the only thing he had left – his own imagination. With his thoughts and dreams in hand, modern man, or as he preferred to be called, "Enlightened" man, seized the opportunity to be his own god and create his own utopia. He turned to machines, technology and the "mechanization of man" to usher in the twentieth century as mankind's finest hour.

Yet, for all her many vital inventions and conveniences, the twentieth century has given man less of what he needs most – *time.* Time to contemplate his existence and what it means to be fully human. Time to examine "higher truths" and "the deep things of the soul." Time to understand the relationship between Creator and creature. Time to cultivate the art of silence and true leisure. Instead, machines and technology made modern man a slave to his own myth of progress – "bigger, faster, more." In his prophetic work entitled, *The Pilgrim's Regress*, C. S. Lewis defined modern man's version of "progress" in the

83

following manner. "Their labor-saving devices multiply drudgery, their aphrodisiacs make them impotent, their amusements bore them, their rapid production of food leaves half of them starving, and their devices for saving time have banished leisure from their country."[122] One thing painfully obvious about 'modern progress' is that we all are much busier now than we ever used to be. All these timesaving devices have done exactly the opposite of saving time: they've killed time, or enslaved us to time...[123]

Josef Pieper, in his philosophical masterpiece from 1948 entitled, *Leisure: The Basis of Culture*, brilliantly presents the moral imperative for a proper understanding of individual and societal leisure. As stated in Gerald Malsbary's recent translation, "Leisure is an attitude of mind and a condition of the soul that fosters a capacity to perceive the reality of the world. Religion (and philosophy) can be born only in leisure – a leisure that allows time for the contemplation of the nature of God. Leisure has been, and always will be, the first foundation of any culture. In our bourgeois Western world, total labor has vanquished leisure. Unless we regain the art of silence and insight, the ability for non-activity, unless we substitute true leisure for our hectic amusements, we will destroy our culture – and ourselves."[124]

Sadly, instead of returning to simplicity and the contemplation of truth, postmodern man stubbornly entered the twentieth century fixated on his own cleverness and independence. How did it turn out? Suffice is to say that as we enter into the third millennium, we must never forget that we do so only

---

[122] Peter Kreeft, *C. S. Lewis for the Third Millennium* (San Francisco, Ignatius Press, 1994), 23-24.

[123] Peter Kreeft, *C. S. Lewis for the Third Millennium* (San Francisco, Ignatius Press, 1994), 55.

[124] Josef Pieper, *Leisure: The Basis of Culture* (South Bend, St. Augustine's Press, 1998), cover.

after murdering more people in this past century than in all previous centuries *combined*. Author Bradley Birzer, in his timely book, *J.R.R. Tolkien's Sanctifying Myth*, appropriately suggests that the twentieth century – having traded absolute truth and standards for individual whim – will not be remembered for achievement, but for wholesale destruction and death. Birzer writes, "The mechanization of man and nature revealed its full diabolical potential in the statist crimes committed during the twentieth century...Considering the death and brutality littering its landscape, it is hard to admire much in the century just passed." He continues, "From the beginning of recorded history to 1900, governments murdered an estimated 133 million of their own citizens. Between 1901 and 1987, governments killed nearly 170 million of their own citizens. Stalin slaughtered 41 million, Mao 35 million, and Hitler 21 million. Another 38.5 million died in state-sponsored wars during the same period. When some demographer gets around to making the final count for the century, including those killed in Africa, the former Yugoslavia, and China since 1987, the figure may push beyond 200 million."[125] The reader should also consider that I have only included the statistics dealing with political regimes – I did not *even* include the tally of untold millions of lives from the most defenseless of all categories of human beings, unborn babies.

It should not go unnoticed that post-modern man, despite these statistics, continues to embrace relativistic thinking and look down his nose at the "outdated" absolutist philosophies of the ancient and medieval era's. Convinced, for example, that man does not posses an inner law or moral compass to govern his behavior, modern and post-modern thinkers concluded that humanity must be governed by man-

---

[125] Bradley Birzer, *J.R.R. Tolkien's Sanctifying Myth* (Wilmington, ISI Books, 2003), 113-114.

made doctrines. Still, in recent years, all the grand propositions advanced over the past (twentieth) century have fallen, one by one, like toy soldiers. The twentieth century was the age of ideology, of the great "isms": Communism, socialism, Nazism, liberalism, scientism...But today all the major ideological constructions are being tossed on the ash heap of history. All that remains is the cynicism of postmodernism, with its bankrupt assertions that there is no objective truth or meaning, that we are free to create our own truth as long as we understand that it is nothing more than a subjective dream, a comforting illusion.[126] Professor Bradley Birzer, rightly suggests that, "Instead of trying to force real, living, historically rooted human beings to fit the abstract imaginings of ideologies, man must live within and order himself according to the natural law (absolute truth)." He continues that this is something that the ancient and brilliant political philosopher Cicero understood when he wrote, "True law is right reason in agreement with nature; it is of universal application, unchanging and everlasting; it summons to duty by its commands, and averts from wrongdoing by its prohibitions...It is a sin to try to alter this (natural) law, nor is it allowable to attempt to repeal any part of it, and it is impossible to abolish entirely...And there will not be different laws...now and in the future, but one eternal and unchangeable law will be valid for all nations and all times, and there will be one master and ruler, that is, God, over us all, for he is the author of this (natural) law, its promulgator, and its enforcing judge."[127]

As I come to a close, I am reminded of something Plato once said. When asked why society

---

[126] Chuck Colson, *How Now Shall We Live?* (Wheaton, Tyndale House, 1999), 303.
[127] Bradley Birzer, *J.R.R. Tolkien's Sanctifying Myth* (Wilmington, ISI Books, 2003), 134.

should bother with education, he replied, "We should educate people so that they become good people, because good people behave nobly." Similarly, in his classic work, *Nicomachean Ethics*, Aristotle stated, "The ultimate purpose in studying ethics (philosophy) is not as it is in other inquiries, the attainment of theoretical knowledge; we are not conducting this inquiry in order to know what virtue is, but in order to become good, else there would be no advantage in studying it."

In the film, *Tuesday's With Morrie*, a dying professor is asked how one can find the meaning of life. The frail and gentle teacher replies, "When you know how to die, you know how to live." When we study "THE BIG PICTURE" and ask questions of ourselves and our universe, we begin to understand what Morrie meant. Like Victor Frankl, we soon realize that *Truth* is teaching us the ultimate existential lesson: "That it does not really matter what we expect from life, but rather what life expects from us. We need to stop asking about the meaning of life, and instead to think of ourselves as those who were being questioned by life – daily and hourly. Our answer must consist, not in talk and meditation, but in right action and in right conduct."

Continuing with an emphasis on individual accountability, Frankl writes, "A human being is not one thing among other; *things* determine each other, but *man* is ultimately self-determining. What he becomes – within the limits of endowment and environment – he has made out of himself. In the concentration camps, for example, in this living laboratory and on this testing ground, we watched and witnessed some of our comrades behave like swine while others behaved like saints. Man has both potentialities within himself; which one is actualized depends on decisions but not on conditions. Our generation is realistic, for we have come to know man as he really is. After all, man is that being who invented the gas chambers of Auschwitz;

however, he is also that being who entered those gas chambers upright, with the Lord's Prayer or the *Shema Yisrael* on his lips."[128]

Pleasure, freedom, happiness, prosperity – none of these is ultimately fulfilling because none can answer that ultimate question of *purpose*. What is the purpose of human life?...Which worldview (absolutism or relativism) provides a sense of assurance about our ultimate destiny? Every view of human life is shaped by two great assumptions: our origin and our destiny – where we came from and where we are going. The latter asks, Is this life all there is? Is death the end of all our deepest aspirations and longings? The (secular) existentialist pointed out that if there is nothing beyond the grave, then death makes a mockery of everything we have lived for; death reduces human projects and dreams to a temporary diversion, with no ultimate significance. *But* if our souls survive beyond the grave, as the Bible teaches, then this life is invested with profound meaning. Everything we do here has a significance for all eternity. The life of each person, whether in the womb or out, whether healthy or infirm, takes on an enormous dignity.[129] That, in the end, is THE BIG PICTURE!

---

[128] Victor Frankl, *Man's Search for Meaning* (New York, Washington Square Press, 1959), 98, 137.
[129] Chuck Colson, *How Now Shall We Live?* (Wheaton, Tyndale House, 1999), 135.